FRUGAL FRESH START

A 28-day challenge to trim your
expenses, build a budget &
fix your finances

By Stephanie Jones

Disclaimer

The information in this book is based on the author's opinion, knowledge, and experience. The author will not be held liable for the use or misuse of the information contained herein.

Table of Contents

Introduction

Do you feel like you'll never get ahead financially? Has living from paycheck to paycheck made you feel hopeless? Do you want to get started paying off debt or make headway on your savings goals, but just don't know where to start?

You're in the right place!

By the end of *Frugal Fresh Start*, you will have trimmed your expenses in effective and practical ways, leaving money in your hands. Those savings will no longer get lost in the shuffle! With your new budget, built especially for your personal style and financial situation, your money will be actively working to help you reach your goals. If those goals include paying off debt, you'll gain a plan for tackling that, along with some serious momentum.

Your only regret will be that you didn't do this sooner!

The Challenge

Frugal Fresh Start is neatly organized into 28 days where you'll learn the basics of budgeting, living frugally, and getting your finances in order. Each day includes a challenge to help you apply the day's principle in a practical and meaningful way.

While this is a 28-day challenge, you probably can't expect to be finished fixing your finances in the four weeks you take on the challenge. You absolutely can expect to have formed a great foundation of strong principles of frugal living and practical opportunities to implement those principles and build yourself a frugal and fulfilling financial life.

A Warning

Don't try to read the whole book in one sitting. It is designed to be digested one day at a time, giving time for you to merge each idea into your thoughts and your personal routine.

Reading this book straight through will be overwhelming. That's not the way to have a frugal fresh start. Building habits takes time. If you really want to make lasting financial changes, do yourself the favor of taking this challenge one day at a time. You'll be glad you did!

This Book is For YOU!

The challenges in this book are adaptable to the level of intensity you are willing and able to bring to them. Whether you're just getting started with a frugal lifestyle or you want to recommit to being more frugal, *Frugal Fresh Start* will help you revamp your finances and make strides toward your goals.

Because this book focuses on principles and challenges rather than just tips and tricks, every chapter can apply to YOU in a meaningful way. Start from where you are right now. Fretting about yesterday is neither productive nor encouraging. Leave it behind you and start fresh today.

Are you ready to form new frugal habits and get your finances in order?

Great! Let's do this!

Day 1: Turn Your "Why" Into a Goal

Welcome to the Frugal Fresh Start Challenge! Each day includes a specific challenge to help you make new frugal habits, lower your expenses, and get your finances in order.

Why do you want to be more frugal?

To get started, let's think about YOUR reason to make a frugal fresh start. It's probably not just for the fun of it, or to get attention from your friends. Maybe you want to pay off those credit cards once and for all. Maybe you want to save for a house. Maybe your retirement accounts are slimmer than you'd like. Maybe you just have a spending problem. Who couldn't use a little more cash in their pockets?

Let's turn your reason into a goal.

I love this metaphor from Earl Nightingale.

> *"People with goals succeed because they know where they're going. It's that simple. Failures, on the other hand, believe that their lives are shaped by circumstances ... by things that happen to them ... by exterior forces.*
>
> *Think of a ship with the complete voyage mapped out and planned. The captain and crew know exactly where the ship is going and how long it will take—it has a definite goal. And 9,999 times out of 10,000, it will get there.*
>
> *Now let's take another ship, just like the first, only let's not put a crew on it, or a captain at the helm. Let's give it no aiming point, no goal, and no destination. We just start the engines and let it go. I think you'll agree that if it gets out of the harbor at all, it will either*

sink or wind up on some deserted beach–a derelict. It can't go anyplace because it has no destination and no guidance."

It's very hard to succeed unless you know what you're trying to succeed at. If you're not trying to reach a defined destination, your end point will be determined by a series of uncoordinated decisions made each time you find yourself under pressure. Your goal is your destination. It's where you want to end up. It keeps you from simply wandering.

A goal does three things for you:

1. It gives you a direction and helps you focus your efforts to make sure you're heading in that direction.

2. It acts as a finish line, a destination that you look to for motivation when things get hard.

3. It allows you to measure and celebrate your progress.

Goals come in all shapes and sizes. Goals can be hourly (keep the peace until bedtime) or span years (pay off student loans). For the purpose of this challenge, I want you to set a goal for about 6 months down the road.

What sort of a goal? That depends on you! Think of your reason for wanting a frugal fresh start and you may find that you have a goal already, or at least the beginnings of one. To get your mind moving, here is a non-comprehensive list of examples that could be a goal or part of a goal, in no particular order:

• Save a certain amount of money for a certain purpose (new car, vacation, down payment, retirement).

• Quit spending on certain items altogether.

• Constrain spending in certain categories in a measurable way.

• Pay off a certain credit card balance.

- Pay off a certain portion (either amount or percentage) of some other debt.

- Add a certain amount to an emergency fund.

- Make three extra mortgage payments.

Don't get so caught up in the right number for your goal right now, especially if being actively involved in your finances is new for you. The actual number may need adjusting after you begin, but having some number is important. If your goal is not quantifiable, you won't be able to tell if you're making progress, and at the end of six months, you won't know if you succeeded!

The most important part is to set a goal that will motivate you and give you a reason to be more frugal. A good goal will help you realize that the sacrifices you are making and the new habits you are cultivating will be worth it.

Day 1 Challenge

Set a financial goal for 6 months from now that gives you a reason to be more frugal. Write your goal down in a place where you will see it.

Note: If you're anything like me, you're about to turn the page and read Day 2.

DON'T DO IT!

This book is not a novel that can be read and digested in a day or two. While Day 1 has a pretty simple challenge, they will get more involved, and it takes time to let each day's idea and challenge work. To have a really successful frugal fresh start, take one day at a time or at most, combine a few of the easier consecutive days. Now, slowly, put the book down, go decide on your goal, and write it down. Let's talk again tomorrow.

Day 2: Cut Something Quick!

We're going to get a jump-start on our goal by choosing something to cut out right now, for the rest of the month. Even before we get into tracking spending, budgeting, or cutting expenses, I'm pretty sure you can think of a couple of areas right off the bat that you could trim down or eliminate completely. Maybe as you set your goal yesterday your mind has already started churning through some possible expenses you could cut.

Maybe gourmet coffee is your guilty pleasure. Maybe you eat out too often. Maybe browsing eBay inevitably results in unnecessary spending. In case you're drawing a blank, here are some possibilities:

- Cut out fast food

- Cancel cable

- Spend $0 on entertainment

- Cut out meat

- Give up treats

- Spend $0 on clothes

- Cancel your gym membership and run instead

- Stay out of Target (or whatever your shopping weakness is)

Just choose one. You don't have to commit to dropping the expense forever, just for the month of the Frugal Fresh Start Challenge. If cutting something completely and cold-turkey is overwhelming, make specific limitations on how you will cut back. For example, if you eat out most nights, cut back to only eating out twice a week.

Calculate Your Savings

Do a little multiplication to figure out how much your initial sacrifice will save you this month. How about if you cut the expense for the whole year? Seeing how much your sacrifice is saving you can really motivate you to keep it up.

For example, if you stop by Starbucks on your way to work five days a week and spend $3 a day, you will save $15 a week or $60 a month by ditching the Starbucks habit. A $3 per weekday habit will save you more than $700 over the course of a year! Think of what else you could do with that money!

If you have a weakness for a certain website or store, do you know how much you spend there in a typical month? Take a look at the last two or three months and see how much you have spent. Average those months together to get an idea of how much you will save by swearing off that shopping temptation for the month.

Attitude is Everything

As the month goes on and you start to feel the pain of the expense you amputated from your budget, remember that you chose to cut this expense. No one made you do it.

Instead of turning down your friend by saying "Sorry, I can't eat out this month," consider being pro-active and taking ownership of your choice. You could say, "I've decided not to spend money eating out this month" or "I have an awesome financial goal I'm working toward this month, so I'm not spending money on restaurants."

No one wants to feel like the victim of their budget. Reminding yourself that you are making a choice to improve your financial situation and reach your goals will help you stay positive and feel empowered.

Day 2 Challenge

Choose an expense to cut right now. It doesn't have to be a lifetime commitment, just one month. The important thing is to decide and begin today!

Day 3: Track Your Spending

You have a 6-month goal and you've made a quick start by cutting out one expense for the rest of the month. Day 3 of the Frugal Fresh Start Challenge starts a habit that is essential to improving finances – meticulously tracking your spending.

I don't think there is anything more critical to personal financial success than really understanding where your money goes every month. Even people who think they have a good idea of how they spend their money end up being surprised when they carefully track spending and add everything up.

> *"Measurement is the first step that leads to control and eventually to improvement. If you can't measure something, you can't understand it. If you can't understand it, you can't control it. If you can't control it, you can't improve it." – James Harrington*

Most of us know we could do better with our spending, but until you know exactly how much you spend on what, you don't have enough information to see clearly. If you can't see your spending clearly, you can't choose to make the most effective changes in your spending habits.

Some expenses are overlooked because they happen automatically. Others don't seem significant until you aggregate a month's worth of individually small transactions. Whether it's seeing how much you really spend on eating out, or what parking fees actually amount to, or how much groceries actually cost, tracking your spending in detail is always an eye-opener.

Start From Today

Don't bother back-tracking. Just start from today. Trying to recreate past spending is frustrating and unproductive. Start fresh today.

Write down everything you spent today, including cash purchases, checks, online purchases, automatic withdrawals, and bill-pay. Everything!

Then do it again tomorrow.

The easiest way to track expenses is also the simplest – get a pad of lined paper, write the month at the top, and add one expenditure per line for every expense of the month.

If you're comfortable with Excel or another spreadsheet program, a spreadsheet is just the electronic version of lined paper. You don't need any fancy tools to track spending, just the commitment to actually do it every day.

Categorize Carefully

You can put each expense into a category. Be meticulous about your categorizing. Avoid categories like "shopping," "miscellaneous," or other catch-alls that don't force you to analyze your purchases. Knowing that you spend $300 last month on miscellaneous things isn't very telling. You really need to know where your money is going in order to improve your financial habits and be more frugal. We'll get more into categories next week when we start in on budgeting, but for now, just be careful not to be overly broad in your categories.

Be careful of using programs like Mint to categorize for you. When you start paying attention, you'll realize that Mint actually doesn't do a very good job of categorizing your spending. You can still use Mint to track spending if you like, just don't count on it being as automated as you think. You will need to manually adjust the categories for many transactions. It's pretty hilarious sometimes to see Mint guess at the expense category.

While it is convenient to have transactions automatically appear like they do in Mint, real awareness of your spending habits comes when you write down or manually enter transactions. Not only will you get the category right the first time, but you'll have an intimate relationship with your spending, as it happens, every day.

Expense Tracking Spreadsheet

I created a basic Expense Tracking Spreadsheet that you are welcome to download for free (see the link to resources at the end of the book). There are several sample entries to give you an idea of how it works. You can delete them when you start. I have some common categories already listed, but you can edit them to fit your specific needs. As you will see, I focused on variable expenses, but you can add categories for the fixed expenses as they occur. We will talk about budget categories in detail on Day 6.

Be sure to split transactions that cover more than one category. For example, transactions from Walmart or Target could have groceries, household items, clothes, gifts, or other categories all on the same receipt. People fall into the trap of using categories like "shopping" and "miscellaneous" because they either are too lazy to split up the transaction, or they don't have their receipt to know what they bought. Get in the habit of recording your spending on the day it happens so you don't forget what you bought.

With the way we budget (we'll get there on Day 7), tracking expenses is inseparable from budgeting.

Here are a few tips to help you start tracking your spending:

• Save your receipts until you have recorded the transaction. Looking just at your credit card statement won't tell you what you bought at Walmart.

• Be sure to include online transactions.

• Include automated withdrawals and bill-pay transactions.

• Don't forget to enter cash transactions.

• Do it every day. If you let four days go by, it's much more difficult to recreate your spending. Make a habit of doing it each day before you go to bed.

A Warning

If you've never diligently tracked your spending and you're under the impression that this will be a fun or easy exercise, I warn you that it probably won't be.

You'll have to be meticulous and diligent. Starting new habits is hard.

Also, seeing the actual numbers written down might be discouraging. I promise you it will be worth it to get a clear picture of where your money is going.

The simple act of tracking your spending might even help you curb habits. You might avoid making unnecessary purchases just so you won't have to write them down, either for shame or laziness. If you've ever tracked your food intake for a health class or to improve your diet, you may have noticed this same phenomenon. It's a nice side benefit of tracking your habits.

Day 3 Challenge

Start tracking your spending—every expense, every day—for the rest of the challenge (and hopefully beyond). I simply can't adequately express the importance of this exercise, even for those of us who think we already know all about our expenses.

Day 4: Get Some Accountability

In the Day 1 Challenge, I had you write down your goal. If it's not written down, it's just a wish or a hope. If you didn't actually write down your goal, I'll give you a second chance. You can write it down on a note card and put it in your wallet, on your computer monitor, on your fridge, on your mirror, or wherever you will see it and be inspired by it.

Now that you've written down your goal, let's take it a step further. Telling someone about your goal will solidify it even further. We all feel more committed to a goal when we have told others about it. You don't need to make a public announcement, but choosing a person or two to hold you accountable to your goals will seriously increase your success in achieving them.

Having a buddy or accountability partner goes beyond just having someone hold you accountable to your goals. A good partner will be more than just a taskmaster checking in on your progress. Your buddy, if you find a good one, will encourage you each step of the way.

Buddies in the Same Boat

Several times in my life I have felt motivated to run, not because someone was chasing me, but for fun! One time my husband and I even competed in a triathlon (swimming and biking are more fun than running).

The best training partners are the ones who run alongside you and train with you. You both have similar goals so training together just makes sense. Not only is there accountability, motivation, and encouragement, but it's just more fun.

Finding a buddy who's in the same boat is a great option for help in achieving financial goals too. Do you know someone who is also trying to be more frugal and has set lofty financial goals? Could you both benefit from one another's encouragement and camaraderie? You don't have to share every financial detail with your buddy, just enough about your goals and commitments that you can support and help one another, as well as celebrate one another's success.

Spouses Can be the Best or the Worst

Sometimes a spouse makes a great accountability partner. While your weaknesses and strengths are different, your overall goals (financial and otherwise) should be well-aligned. You should already each be privy to all the ins and outs of your shared finances, which is convenient. You both benefit from successfully accomplishing your goals. Hopefully you have learned to work together as a team. If you are both on board with revamping spending and saving habits and making the necessary changes to reach your goals, then your spouse might make a great accountability partner.

In other cases, closeness can make it too easy to not be your best. For example, if my husband and I have a 6:00 am date to go running, I might complain that I'm tired and try to talk him out of it when the alarm goes off at 5:45. Depending on how tired he is, I might be successful. On the other hand, if I am meeting a friend to run at 6:00 am, you better believe I'll drag my tired self out of bed anyway so I don't let her down.

It may be too easy to justify breaking your goals to your spouse. And of course, if your spouse is not on board with the proposed changes, he or she wouldn't be a great accountability partner.

Day 4 Challenge

Find an accountability partner– it could be your spouse, a relative, a friend, or a co-worker. You want someone with whom you can share your goal and your progress, and someone who will be a buddy to encourage you and keep you honest along the way. With your lofty goals, you will need support and encouragement not just this month, but until you reach those goals! Share your goal with your accountability partner.

Day 5: Cook at Home

Do you know what one of the most shocking expense categories that people discover when they start really tracking their expenses is?

It's food.

Between grocery trips throughout the week, eating out for convenience and entertainment, and grabbing snacks at vending machines and gas stations, food expenses add up quickly. If you don't keep track of how much you spend, you might be in for a rude awakening.

Part of becoming more frugal is changing our habits—and that's not always easy. Today we're going to make an effort at reducing our food budget by cooking at home.

Don't tune me out or skip this day because you think you're not good in the kitchen or you're too busy to cook at home. Increasing how much you cook at home is possible for everyone.

With some practice and some adaptations, you can make cooking at home work for you. It's not only good for your wallet; it's also good for your body.

Address Your Concerns

This may sound a little backward, but before we actually make a plan for cooking at home more often, I want you to think about what has kept you from doing so in the past. What are the reasons you end up eating out or ordering take-out?

Addressing these concerns as you make your plan will prevent you from using these excuses or allowing old habits to creep in. Be honest with yourself.

Here are a few common reasons people don't cook at home.

- I'm too busy.

- I don't know how to cook.

- I don't plan ahead.

- I'm tired of the "same old."

As you make a plan, keep your concerns at the front of your mind so you can come up with a way to combat them.

Make a Plan

It's no secret that cooking at home takes more effort and planning than going through a drive-thru or ordering take-out. Knowing what you'll fix before the dinner hour strikes is crucial.

Start by making a list of the dinners you like to cook (or eat), know how to cook, or would like to learn to cook. If you're stumped or are stuck in a menu rut, a simple search on Pinterest will have your mouth watering and your tummy growling for sure. Get some input from your family to make sure their favorites are on the list too.

Look at your calendar and decide how you'll fit the meals in.

If you're new to cooking at home, ease yourself in with a couple of meals to start. If being busy has you eating out often, choose nights where you'll have a little extra time to get used to cooking. As you get more experience under your belt, you'll be able to pull together successful meals more quickly and with less effort.

If you're already in the habit of cooking at home, make out a full menu for the rest of the month. You could even just plan two weeks of meals, then double your plan to last through the month.

Even though I always cook at home, sometimes I am too lazy to follow my own advice and make a menu. Making a menu will save you so much sanity! Having a menu you are excited for and prepared for can put the enjoyment back into cooking at home when you're in a rut or have fallen off the bandwagon.

Prepare

When you have an idea of what you want to make and when you want to make it, schedule a trip to the store to shop for whatever ingredients you don't already have on hand. Look at all your recipes and make a good shopping list so that you only have to make one trip to the store.

If cooking at home is new to you, you will probably have to build up your pantry's stock of staples. For the sake of not getting overwhelmed, try just shopping for a week's worth of meals at a time.

If you're a seasoned family chef, you might want to prepare your menu and shopping list for a longer time period.

If your schedule is busy (or you just like saving time), figure out what prep work you can do ahead of time. Could you chop veggies the morning of or the night before the scheduled meal? Could you prepare several crock pot meals over the weekend and stick them in the freezer? How can you involve your spouse and kids in the preparations?

One of my favorite ways to prepare is to brown my ground beef in bulk (I stretch it with veggies too) when I buy it, then freeze it in meal-sized portions. Getting some of the prep-work out of the way makes fixing dinner a breeze and will prevent you from eating out, even at the end of a long day.

I also have my husband dice a whole bag of onions at a time, which I freeze and use as needed. He barely cries at all.

Combating Challenges

Hopefully thinking about your concerns at the beginning helped you to creatively think through how you personally can overcome the challenges that you face with cooking at home. Figuring out your own solutions is more effective than my giving you all the answers, but in case you still need some hints, here are a few ways to combat the common concerns I listed at the beginning of this chapter:

I'm too busy.

• Use a slow cooker. Your dinner will cook while you are away and will be ready at dinnertime.

• Get a rice cooker with a delay timer. We love this feature on our rice cooker!

• Use weekends to prepare and plan the next week's menu.

• Make enough so you have leftovers. If you don't want the same thing on consecutive days, freeze your leftovers for a busy day.

• Keep meals simple. Your dinner doesn't need to look like a restaurant's spread.

• Enlist your family's help!

I don't know how to cook.

• It's time to learn! There are loads of videos and tutorials available online.

• Start with dishes you love so your motivation will be high.

• Search for simple recipes.

• Learn some versatile basics like soups, salads, and casseroles.

• Get other family members involved.

• Have a freezer cooking day with a friend.

I don't plan ahead.

• Commit to making a menu plan.

• Choose a day each week to plan your menu.

• Plan your shopping trips so you have ingredients on hand.

• Search for freezer meals that can be made now and stored for the days that don't go as planned.

I'm tired of the "same old."

• Challenge yourself to add a new recipe or two to your menu each week.

• Follow some recipe boards on Pinterest to get new ideas.

• Ask your friends on social media to share their favorite go-to recipes.

• Get suggestions from family members.

Day 5 Challenge

Make a plan for cooking and eating at home. Your exact challenge will depend on where you're coming from and what your current habits are. Set a specific goal for remaining 28 days to make some or all of your upcoming meals at home. Find recipes to use and make a shopping list so you won't have any excuses. If your time at home is limited, get to know your slow cooker and get excited about some new recipes. If you already eat at home, choose a couple of new recipes to keep things exciting!

Day 6: Define Budget Categories

It's time to address the B-word. You knew this was coming sooner or later. If "budget" is a bad word in your vocabulary, it's time to fix that! A budget doesn't have to be depressing and restrictive– it can be exciting and freeing!

We actually love our budget! It was exhilarating when we settled on our current process and knew we had something that would really help us manage our financial life intentionally, instead of watching our finances as they went by. We still look forward with excitement to our end-of-the-month budgeting date.

However, putting together a budget all at once can be intimidating, so we'll do this one step at a time. Today we'll start with setting up budget categories. Budget categories need to be personalized to fit your unique financial situation.

If you put some thought into tracking your expenses like we talked about last week, then you've probably already nailed down some good categories for your variable expenses. Today we will build on those variable expenses and add fixed expenses and periodic expenses.

Variable Expenses

Variable expenses are the expenses that change from month-to-month. Most of them don't go away completely, but the amount we spend is never the same each month. We are focusing on variable expenses in our expense tracking report to get a real picture of how we spend our money.

You can use as much or as little detail as you like. The more detail you have, the clearer the picture of where your money is going, but the more work you'll have splitting up those receipts from Target and Walmart.

For example, splitting your grocery purchases up by food group is probably overkill for general budgeting purposes. On the other hand, lumping all of your online purchases into a "shopping" category isn't going to give you enough information to make meaningful changes. You'll find a happy medium that works for you.

Here are some typical categories that you can adapt to your own situation. Make your own rules about what expenses belong in which category. If a new expense comes up that doesn't fit well in your established categories you can add a new category (if it's an expense that will likely recur) or make it fit into an established category (if it was an odd one-time expense). Avoid catch-all categories like "shopping" and "miscellaneous" or use them very sparingly.

- Groceries

- Restaurants

- Gas

- Household

- Baby/Kid Expenses

- Entertainment

- Gifts

- Utilities (gas, electric)

- Cell Phone (if plan varies by usage)

- Medical/Dental Co-Pays

- Prescriptions

- Giving (tithing, charity, etc)

Fixed Monthly Expenses

Fixed expenses are the expenses that don't change from month to month. You know exactly how much those costs will be. You also know the dates that these expenses will be due or will be automatically taken out of your checking account.

Here are some examples of fixed monthly expenses. Some may not apply to you (or they may be periodic or variable rather than fixed monthly expenses) and there are likely other fixed monthly expenses that are not on this list.

- Mortgage/Rent

- Health Insurance

- Dental/Vision Insurance

- Car Insurance

- Home Owner's or Renter's Insurance

- Cable or other TV Subscription

- Phone

- Cell Phone

- HOA Fees

- Debt Payments

- Utilities (electric, trash, internet)

Periodic Expenses

Periodic expenses are ones that come less often than monthly. They could be expenses that come up annually or at some other interval.

Periodic expenses sometimes sneak up on us because they occur so infrequently that we don't have them on our radar.

Once again, this isn't an exhaustive list of possible periodic expenses. Some of these expenses may be fixed monthly or variable expenses in your individual case. Think hard to come up with all of your periodic expenses.

- Life Insurance Premiums

- Car Registration

- Magazine Subscriptions

- Car Insurance

- Property Taxes

- Club or Association Fees

- Domain Registration Renewals

- Tuition

- Membership Fees/ Annual Passes

- Travel

Day 6 Challenge

Define categories for your budget. To help with organization, divide your categories into variable expenses, fixed monthly expenses, and periodic expenses, or in a different way that works for your personal situation. We will use these categories tomorrow when we continue with setting up a fresh budget!

Day 7: Set Your Budget

If you've done any budgeting in the past, it's most likely been of the traditional sort. A traditional budget is characterized by a list of categories, each with an assigned amount of money you plan to spend in that category. Your budget is based on your projected income for the month, which hopefully is more than the total of all the expenses.

Essentially, a traditional budget is a plan of how you will spend the money that you hope to get that month.

We have failed dismally every time we've tried to live by a budget of this sort. These budgets are a chore, and the most frequent emotion they engender is a sort of lingering guilt.

Our actual spending never quite matched our budgeted amounts and we constantly felt like we had failed and should have been better at projecting our expenses or our income. We sometimes found ourselves gerrymandering purchases into unnatural budget categories, as if the budget were an unchangeable fact we had to conform to. We avoided reviewing the budget together, and eventually, just stopped using it completely. It didn't matter if the actual budgeting tool were a sheet of paper, a spreadsheet, or a program like Quicken or Mint, it was always a bad experience.

With a traditional budget there were no built-in restraints or safeguards to ensure that our spending followed our budget. There were no checks to ensure that our spending money had even been earned yet. The rigidity of traditional budgeting methods left us feeling like failures at worst, and unenthusiastic participants at best.

Moving Away From Traditional Budgeting

The best thing that ever happened to our budget was to move away from the traditional budgeting model and adopt a forward-looking budget methodology called YNAB (You Need a Budget). We actually love budgeting now, and can't wait for our end-of-the-month budgeting date each month.

Because I really believe that it is the most effective way, I'm going to lead you through starting your fresh budget in this non-traditional, yet intuitive process. If you've never budgeted before, you won't know the difference. If you have budgeted in the past, you'll probably wonder why you never thought to do it like this before.

Most traditional budgeting software and philosophies look *backwards* at what happened. They analyze where your money went after it's too late to do anything about it. Instead, you'll look *forward*. You'll assign your real, actual money to categories before you spend it.

I'm going to walk you through the steps of setting up your budget using my screenshots from YNAB. Even if you without YNAB, you can still apply the same budgeting rules and methodology to your own spreadsheet. It works wonderfully.

Fund Your Budget

When you start your budget in YNAB, you'll add your checking account balance. You can find the balance of all of your accounts on the left. Since you're just starting out, all the money will go into the "available to budget" number at the top of the month's column. In the future, each time you enter income, you will see money appear at the top of your budget, ready to be budgeted.

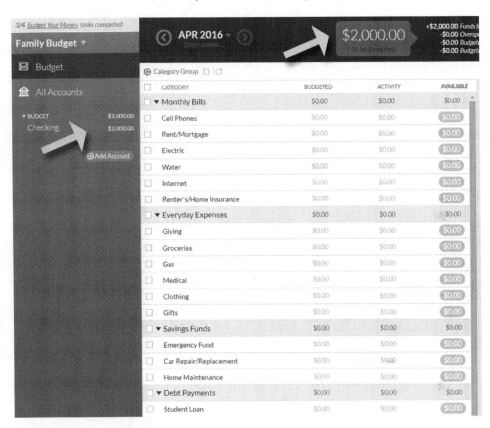

In the above example we have just entered our checking account which has a current balance of $2,000. That money goes straight up to the top to be budgeted.

Budget the Money You Have

You want to tell each of your dollars what to do. Instead of just being a lump of money in your checking account, your money will be earmarked for specific categories. Don't worry, you'll be able to change your allocations when you need to (we'll talk about this on Day 14). You'll budget down to zero, meaning every dollar in your checking account will have a specific "job" or category that it is assigned to. It's like a virtual envelope system.

Giving every dollar a job also means that you are only budgeting money that you already have. You're dealing with money that actually exists, not money that you hope materializes this month. Your budget is a real live animal. It means something!

Start by allocating the money you have in your checking account right now. Decide what you need that money to accomplish before you get paid again. Maybe you'll need to get groceries and gas, and pay the electric bill before your next paycheck. Or maybe there's a rent payment, groceries, and a wedding gift to purchase.

Allocate how much money you think you'll need to each purchase category. If you have a big payment due later in the month, like rent or a mortgage payment, you will probably want to allocate part of the money you have to that category. You'll have to prioritize your categories (i.e. fund your "rent" category before your "fun" category).

Day 7: Set Your Budget

	CATEGORY	BUDGETED	ACTIVITY	AVAILABLE
☐ ▼	Monthly Bills	$1,205.00	$0.00	$1,205.00
☐	Rent/Mortgage	$1,000.00	$0.00	$1,000.00
☐	Electric	$100.00	$0.00	$100.00
☐	Water	$30.00	$0.00	$30.00
☐	Internet	$45.00	$0.00	$45.00
☐	Renter's/Home Insurance	$0.00	$0.00	$0.00
☐	Cell Phones	$30.00	$0.00	$30.00
☐ ▼	Everyday Expenses	$555.00	$0.00	$555.00
☐	Giving	$200.00	$0.00	$200.00
☐	Groceries	$200.00	$0.00	$200.00
☐	Gas	$75.00	$0.00	$75.00
☐	Medical	$50.00	$0.00	$50.00
☐	Clothing	$30.00	$0.00	$30.00
☐	Gifts	$0.00	$0.00	$0.00
☐ ▼	Savings Funds	$200.00	$0.00	$200.00
☐	Emergency Fund	$200.00	$0.00	$200.00
☐	Car Repair/Replacement	$0.00	$0.00	$0.00
☐	Home Maintenance	$0.00	$0.00	$0.00
☐ ▼	Debt Payments	$40.00	$0.00	$40.00
☐	Student Loan	$40.00	$0.00	$40.00

In the example above, we have allocated all the money that was "to be budgeted" into the various categories (long highlighted rectangle) where we plan to spend it. Notice that even though our "to be budgeted" is $0, all of our money is still in our checking account (left side) because we haven't spent it yet.

Maybe you aren't living paycheck-to-paycheck, so some of the money in your checking account is earmarked for your emergency fund or your life insurance premiums. That's great. Just put that money in the appropriate category and it will be accounted for and there to use when you need it.

Each time you get paid, you will allocate money to your various categories. In order to stop the paycheck-to-paycheck cycle, you'll want to start setting aside money to build up a "buffer" that will allow you to live on last month's income. When you have a month's worth of income saved up, you can budget the entire next month using the sum you saved while you direct all your income during the current month to the following month. Your "to be budgeted" money will be based on the money you earned the month before. It is a wonderfully freeing feeling to have a buffer. I can't recommend it highly enough.

Spend According to Your Category Balances

To make your budget work, you need to spend according to the balance in your budget categories. Before making a purchase, check your category balances and make sure that there is sufficient money in the category to cover the purchase. Each time you spend money, record your expenditures either on the mobile app or on your desktop.

Each budget account (checking account, savings account, credit card, etc) will have its own register of transactions. To record spending or income, click on the account on the left side to pull up the register, which looks like this:

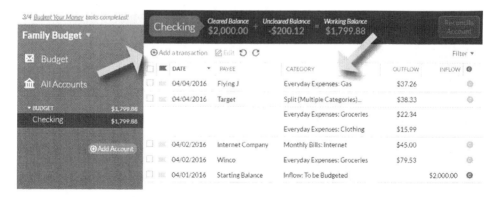

Click on "add new transaction" to add spending or income to the account. You will add a category to each entry.

Since you'll be adding a category to all of your spending transactions, the expense will be subtracted from the category balance in the budget view (see below). Your category balance will show the real "live" amount of money you have available.

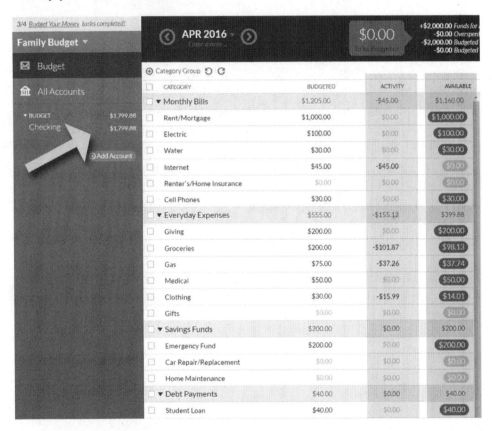

In the "activity" column (highlighted in orange), you can see the spending we've done. The "available" category (highlighted in blue) is the column we want to consult before spending money. It shows us the balance of the funds that category. Our spending is also reflected in the checking account balance on the left.

Even if you're using a credit card to pay for the expense, you will still spend according to the available category balances. Then, when your credit card bill comes, you can be absolutely certain that the money will be sitting in the bank waiting for you to apply it to the credit card. Budgeting like this has taken the stress away from using credit cards for us and left only the benefits.

Safety and Simplicity

There is no need to open specific accounts for special budget goals. You don't have to fret that your new car savings and your property tax money live together with your grocery money and utility expenses in your checking account. Your special savings categories are not in danger of being spent because you will no longer consult your checking account before making purchases. Instead you'll look at the category balances before deciding to make a purchase. As long as you spend according to your categories and track your expenses, you can trust that your money will be safe from accidental (or intentional) spending without having to move your money around between accounts.

I also recommend manually entering data into your budget. While it may be convenient when apps and software automatically grab all your transaction information, there is real value in doing it yourself. You'll see that this manual entry gives awareness and accountability that will bring success.

Day 7 Challenge

Set up a budget either in your own spreadsheet, on paper, or give YNAB a try (it's free for 34 days) using the categories you outlined yesterday. Use the money you have right now to fund your budget, starting with the most urgent categories. Do your best to spend according to your category balances. Be prepared to continue funding categories the next time you get paid.

Bonus Challenge: If you decide to try YNAB, I recommend signing up to watch the "Getting Started with YNAB" class. If you can't actually attend the class, don't worry; they will email you a recorded version. It's a great introduction to the software and methodology. Even if you're using your own spreadsheet, attending a class will help you understand the budgeting philosophy that has made all the difference for us.

Day 8: Lower Your Bills

What's the first budget line you look at when you look for ways to lower your expenses? Most people focus first on the variable expenses like food, entertainment, and gas. That's understandable since those aren't the kind of expenses we call "fixed."

The truth is that some of those "fixed" expenses aren't as fixed as we think. With a little creativity, some research, and willingness to ask, you can lower your monthly bills.

Do Your Research

Competition is a great thing for the consumer. If you have competing service providers in your area, use this to your advantage. Competitors want your business and are willing to pay for it, often by advertising great deals for new customers. You see this frequently with cable packages or internet service plans that are deeply discounted for new customers.

Do some research to find out the going rates and current offers of the various companies in your area. For each of your fixed expenses, call your provider's competitors. Find out their rates and the services they offer. Also, ask about any specials they have for new customers. Take good notes so your conversations don't all get jumbled in your head.

Just Ask

If you are satisfied with your current service, you can first try to work with them on lowering their rates. We have found that many companies are willing to make accommodations in order to keep their loyal customers.

Let the company know you are a satisfied customer and would like to keep their service, but you have noticed that company X is offering a very tempting deal for new customers and you were wondering if they could match that deal. Your script will depend on the information your research uncovers. They have built-in wiggle room in their rates, so companies often are able to work with you on the price.

If you live in an area without much competition, you can still lower your bills by asking. If you have been a faithful customer for any length of time, you could call and let them know that and ask if you can have your rate lowered for being a loyal customer. Especially when faced with the chance of losing you as a customer, companies will respond. If you are considering dropping the service altogether, you can honestly let them know that you are planning to cancel your service if you can't get a lower rate.

Keep in mind that you will have the most success by being honest, patient, and polite.

Don't Be Afraid to Switch

Sometimes we just get in the habit of paying our bills without thinking twice about them. Sometimes we know we are overpaying, but we're too lazy to do anything about it.

Now is the time to do something about it! Remember that goal!

If there is a better deal out there, don't be afraid to switch! You will thank yourself each month for the savings.

In 2014 we made the leap to switch cell phone companies. Giving Republic Wireless a try was a no-brainer for us. Not only do they have a 30-day money-back guarantee, but they also don't do contracts (no signing away your cellular freedom for 2 years at a time). We really didn't have anything to lose. We knew that the prices were unbeatable (unlimited talk, text and WiFi data for $10/mo) and for cell network data you choose what tier you want to pay for, then you actually get refunded for whatever data you don't use.

We've shared our experience with numerous friends, family, and blog readers, and many have also made the switch. I constantly get messages thanking me for pointing them to Republic Wireless because it has saved them so much money. You'll find links to some blog posts about Republic Wireless on my Resources Page.

Question Everything

The best way to go about this exercise is to question each of your monthly expenses. All of your bills are up for negotiation.

Refinancing your home might even be a viable option. You might even consider selling your expensive car and buying a less expensive one. You won't know without making the effort to do the research and weigh the pros and cons.

Write down a list of all the bills that you pay. Look over your budget categories lists that you made on Day 6 as a reminder.

I recommend taking a thorough inventory/audit of your rates at least once a year.

You may even find that some expenses can be cut out completely. While cable might seem like a necessity, cutting out cable indefinitely or even just for a set period of time can really add some momentum to your financial goals.

You Can Do It!

The best part about lowering your monthly bills is that you can take advantage of the savings each month! Even lowering one of your bills by just $10 will save you $120 in a year's time. That's a pretty good payout for a little research and a few minutes on the phone.

Day 8 Challenge

Take a look at each of your fixed expenses with new eyes and think of how you could lower your bills. Do the research, ask questions, be creative, and don't be afraid to make changes.

Day 9: Save Money on Utilities

Sometimes we chalk up utility bills as one of those monthly costs that we don't have control over. We don't see the cost with every use. When we're shopping, we can put something back if the total is too high or we can choose to return items later. Once energy is used, on the other hand, there's no going back. We'll be billed for the use.

Do you know how much your utility bills are each month? Do you pay attention? Because utility bills feel like they're out of our hands, many people pay them blindly without a second thought as to how they can lower those bills.

The truth is, there are quite a few changes you can make to your habits and your home that will save you money. There are even great programs that savvy energy-users can take advantage of to decrease their costs even more.

Are you ready to take matters into your own hands and save money on utilities?

Turn it Off!

I am constantly surprised how often I see people leaving all the lights on in their house, or leaving the TV on when they aren't even in the room, or leaving the water in the kitchen sink running while they rummage through the fridge. If you didn't grow up in a home with energy-conscious parents, then you probably have some long-held habits that are increasing your bills.

The first step to tackling utility bills is being more conscious of our usage. Much of it is a change of mindset and learning to be more aware. Here are a few ideas to keep yourself (and your family) in check and to help build new habits:

• Turn out the lights when you leave the room.

• Turn off the TV if you aren't watching it.

• Turn off fans, lights, TV, music, and computers when you leave the house.

• Before going to bed each night, make sure all lights and screens are off.

Other Great Ideas

The list of ways to save energy could go on and on. It's safe to say that there is room for improvement in every household. Here are some ideas to get your wheels spinning. What ways can you reduce your energy usage and save money on utilities?

• Regularly change your HVAC air filters. Your system will work more efficiently which saves energy and you'll also prolong the life of your system. Better yet, use reusable filters that can be cleaned instead of thrown away!

• Dry your clothes on a clothesline. Appliances with a heating element are energy suckers. Harness the power of the sun to dry your clothes instead.

• Get a programmable thermostat. Put your heating and cooling on autopilot so you're not heating or cooling the house when you're not there. For as little as about $20, you can save up to 33% off your energy bill (if used as directed).

• Prevent air leaks. According to energy.gov, if you put all the air leaks in a house together it would be the equivalent of leaving a 2 ft by 2 ft window open all year. Yikes! Install some foam caulking or weather stripping around doorways. Insulate around where pipes enter the house. If new windows aren't in the budget, window insulator kits do an excellent job!

• Open and close your windows and shades. In the winter, take advantage of the warm sun shining through your windows. On cool summer nights, open windows to cool down your house. Get in the habit of using natural heating and cooling methods instead of turning on the air and heat.

• Dress appropriately. Our secret to keeping heating bills low is to dress for the weather and wait as long as possible to turn on the heat. When we do turn on the heat we keep the thermostat low. In the summer we do the reverse.

• Prepare your home for vacations. Before going out of town, turn your water heater down. Adjust your thermostat so that your heating and cooling won't need to work while you're gone. Unplug appliances since they suck power even when they aren't on.

• Replace incandescent bulbs with CFLs or LEDs. I honestly like the light of incandescent bulbs best, but current incandescent technology does use a lot more energy than CFL or LED bulbs. In California where state law has banned incandescent bulbs, we can choose CFLs or LEDs. CFLs are easy to screw into the fixtures you already have and cheaper to purchase than LEDs. LEDs can cost more upfront but use much less energy don't emit heat, and pretty much never need to be replaced. Some LEDs work well in fixtures made for incandescent bulbs, but not all, and many have problems with dimmers. The surest way to get good LED light is to purchase an LED-specific fixture. For $29, we recently installed one LED fixture at home as a test case and are loving it. Gradually we will change out all our current fixtures.

• Clean out the dryer lint after each load. Your clothes will dry faster and you'll save on energy use when your lint trap is clean allowing your dryer to run more efficiently.

• Conduct a home energy audit. There are professionals that offer this service using specialized equipment, but you can conduct a DIY home energy audit and definitely find some areas where you can improve.

Incentive Programs

When we were in law school, our electric company had a money-saving program where we could choose to have our electric bill calculated at the varying hourly rate (expensive in peak hours, low in non-peak hours) instead of the daily flat rate. By changing our energy usage habits, we saved a lot of money on our electric bill. Each night the rates were published online for the next day. We would avoid running the air conditioner, doing laundry or other high-energy activities during peak hours when the rates were the highest.

Making changes to our energy habits was definitely worth the savings. We had to opt into the program for a year since they invested some start-up costs like installing a new hourly meter at our house. Each month our bill would show what we would have paid at the regular flat hourly rate versus the variable hourly rate we got by being in the program. The only regret we had is that we didn't learn about the program sooner! See if your electric company has a program for keeping your usage down at peak hours or a program where the rates vary by time of day.

If your house or major appliances are not energy-efficient, many utility companies and government offices offer incentives to upgrade your appliances or make energy-efficient home improvements. In fact, sometimes the expense is covered entirely! The Office of Energy Efficiency and Renewable Energy has a list of the various incentive programs available in each state. You can also check the Database of State Incentives for Renewables and Efficiency. Click on your state and see what programs are available.

Day 9 Challenge

What can you do to reduce the utility usage at your house? Resolve to make a few changes and see how they impact your bill. Be sure to enlist your family's help in reducing your usage.

Day 10: Pack Your Lunch

After two days in the budgeting trenches, today's topic is a little lighter. We're going to talk about food again, but about lunch this time. If you have a habit of eating out for lunch, grabbing something to eat on the go, or sending your kids with lunch money, then you have loads of money-saving potential in packing your lunch.

If you have mastered the art of packing your lunch (and eating it), then keep up the good work. Keep reading for more ways to maximize the savings for this frugal and healthy habit.

What's Stopping You?

If you aren't already packing your lunch, what's holding you back? Before we talk about practical tips and ideas, we first need to address whatever it is that's keeping you from bringing a sack lunch to work or sending one with your spouse and kids. Are the mornings too rushed? Do you feel you don't have anything to put in lunches? Do PBJs make you cringe? Are you worried about what your co-workers will think?

Have you thought of the obstacle or concern that is preventing you from bringing your lunch or "forcing" you to eat out? Is it a bigger deal than the goal that you set at the beginning of the book? Unless your boss subsidizes all of your lunches out, I'm pretty certain that bringing your lunch will bring you closer to achieving your goal than eating out will. If packing your lunch turns out to be terrible, you can always go back to buying lunch after you reach your goal.

Plan Ahead

Honestly, packing lunches is not my most favorite way to be frugal. If I haven't planned ahead, I dread waking up to pack my kids' and husband's lunches.

When I'm on top of my game, I have lunches packed for my husband and two school-aged kids the night before. Unfortunately I'm not always that organized. I still send lunches with them every day because I can't stomach paying $2.75 for a school lunch. It just means mornings are rushed if I don't plan ahead.

Just like cooking at home (see Day 5), planning ahead is the key to success in packing lunches. When you're in a hurry to rush out the door in the morning is not the time to plan. Here are some tips to help with planning lunches:

• Make sandwiches ahead of time and freeze them! By lunch time they'll be thawed and ready to eat. Don't freeze lettuce or other greens for sandwiches, but meat and cheese, and peanut butter and jelly freeze well.

• Make a list of possible lunch foods and incorporate them into your grocery list.

• Have fresh fruit on hand like bananas, apples, grapes, and oranges (or Cuties). They're so easy to toss into a lunch and are good for you too!

• Don't forget veggies! Carrots and celery sticks can be cut ahead of time and stored in water in your fridge so they don't dry out.

• Plan to make enough dinner to have leftovers to put in lunches. We often make homemade pizza for dinner. We each make our own and eat right off our pan at dinner (the kids love this). For the next day (or two), everyone gets their leftover pizza for lunch.

• Mason jar salads can be made for the whole week. Just put a jar in each day's lunch and you can dump it in a bowl at lunchtime. And they're so pretty too (search "mason jar salad" on Google or Pinterest if you don't know what I'm talking about).

• Divvy up a week's worth of lunch snacks at a time (see first bullet of next section). This is especially helpful if you're making lunch for several people.

Maximize Savings

By packing just about anything, you'll be saving money over going out to eat, but there are ways to save even more money on your sack lunch. Here are some tips:

• Instead of buying individually packaged items that are marketed for lunches, buy a normal sized package and divvy them up into individual packages yourself. Think pretzels, carrots, cookies, mini muffins, etc.

• Reuse sandwich bags. My husband and kids bring home their sandwich bags if they aren't dirty and I use them again. Each bag only costs a penny, but when there are 4-5 in each lunch, it adds up. It's also less waste and one more thing I don't have to remember to buy as frequently.

• Use reusable containers instead of sandwich bags. You may have seen cute Bento box ideas on Pinterest. You don't have to be all cutesy, but you can still use the great compartmentalized containers I love on my recommendations list.

• Yogurt is one of the most marked up prices in the grocery store. We make our own yogurt, which saves so much money. I put the yogurt into leak-proof containers and send along a spoon.

• Stores with closeouts and clearances like Grocery Outlet often have great deals on granola bars and other lunch snacks that are near the "sell by" date, but are usually just fine. I always figure the price per item in order to compare and I'll only by them if they are very inexpensive.

• Individual string cheese can be expensive per ounce (unless I find it at a closeout store), but I can easily cut cheese sticks from a block of cheese instead. You can cut and freeze sticks of cheese too!

• Instead of juice boxes or buying a ridiculously priced 1/2 pint of milk, pack a water bottle. I send my kids with water in a reusable water bottle every day. My husband keeps a water bottle at his desk and in his car. Drinking water not only saves money, it's better for you than pretty much anything else you're drinking and most of us don't drink enough of it!

Now Eat It!

I've learned from my blog readers that even when you bring your lunch with you, there is still a temptation to go out to eat instead of eating the lunch you packed. Your co-workers, who haven't committed to being more frugal to achieve their goals, want company when they take their lunch break.

One reader said that her husband will go out with his co-workers, but will bring and eat his own packed lunch. I thought that was a great example of someone who sticks to his guns and enjoys the best of both worlds.

Try being open with your co-workers about making changes so you can reach your financial goals. You could even challenge *them* to bring their own lunch. Maybe they've never thought about how much money bringing their lunch would save them.

If you've been in the habit of eating out, you could cut back to once or twice a month. Let your friends know that you'll take a raincheck for a lunch date until then.

Whatever you decide, remember that attitude is everything. This is a choice you are making, not a restriction being imposed on you. It's not that you can't afford to eat out, it's that you are choosing to spend your money in a different way. You're not a victim; you're being proactive by making a choice and sticking to it.

Day 10 Challenge

Start packing your lunch! Challenge yourself with a personal goal for how often you will brown bag it, whether it's for you, your spouse, or your children.

Day 11: Assess Your Debt

An important part of getting your budget in order and having a frugal fresh start is getting a handle on any debt that you have. We're actually in the midst of paying off six figures of my husband's law school debt, so this is a topic always on the top of my mind.

If you don't have any debt at all, congratulations! You can skip this chapter and take a day off.

For everyone else, it's time to get all of your debt out in the open. While you can't expect to tackle your entire debt within this 28-day challenge (wouldn't that be a dream!), laying it out on the table and coming up with a rough long-term plan is the first step.

Maybe paying off some of your debt is part of the six-month goal that you set on Day 1. That is great! Now, you want to get a true picture of where you stand regarding debt.

Find out how much you actually owe

If your debt is spread out across multiple debtors, get all the details in one place. Get out a piece of paper or make your own spreadsheet on the computer. You'll want to gather and record the following details about each of your debts:

- Total amount owed

- Interest rate

- Minimum monthly payment

Don't let this discourage you. Let the big picture motivate you to take this frugality thing seriously so you can get yourself to a better place financially.

Make sure you can cover the minimum payments

The first step of your plan is to make a budget and assess your cash flow. The budget that you made on Day 7 should include your minimum payments on each of your debts.

It's important to pay at least the monthly minimum to each of your creditors to avoid penalties. Assuming you have more than one debt, you will want to focus your best effort on one debt at a time until it's eliminated, but you'll need to pay the minimum on all of your debts each month.

Set your self up for success

Before diving straight into a serious debt payoff plan, you'll want an emergency fund in place. An emergency fund allows you to handle financial emergencies that arise without derailing your entire debt payoff plan. With a cushion of money available if you need it, you can have a sense of security, even amidst serious debt. You'll also prevent a tailspin of repeated failures that can be defeating. If you don't already have an emergency fund, focus on building one up as the first step of your debt payoff plan.

A standard starting point for an emergency fund is $1,000, though for most people that is on the low side. I can't tell you what the right number is for you. You'll want to consider factors like what your "emergencies" have looked like in the past and how much your normal expenses total for a month. The size of your emergency fund will also depend on how long you expect your debt payoff to take. If you anticipate a longer debt payoff time frame, you'll want to have more saved. Choose a number that you are comfortable with. There's no right answer.

Make a plan of attack

Now it's time to make your plan of attack for your debt, even if it's a more long-term plan. If you just have one debt, it's easy to know where to start, but if you have multiple debts, you'll have to decide where you want to focus your extra attention.

Snowball Method

The best way to pay off your debt when you have multiple debts is to focus your attention on one of your debts at a time while still keeping up the minimums on all your other debts. Any extra money that you earn or save from other areas in your budget should go toward the one debt that you are focusing on.

When you finish paying off the first debt, take the amount you were paying toward the first debt (minimum payment, plus whatever extra you come up with) and put it toward the second debt. When the second debt is paid off, put the minimum payments from debt one and two toward debt three along with any extra you can come up with.

The idea of focusing on one debt at a time, then rolling the payments from the debts you pay off into the payment for the next debt is generally called the snowball method.

The big question is the order that you will put your debts in. You can order your debts by balance (starting with the smallest), by interest rate (starting with the highest), or use other personal deciding factors.

Balance (Smallest to Largest)

Often, when people speak of the "debt snowball" method, they are talking specifically about ordering their debts by the size of the balance (though any method where payments roll over to the next debt is technically a snowball method). This method has you focus on paying off the smallest debt first, no matter the interest rate.

51

You make minimum payments on all debts, and any additional funds go toward the smallest debt you have. When that smallest debt is paid in full, you take the monthly payment that you were making toward that smallest debt and add it to the next smallest debt.

The main reasons for ordering your debt by balance is that you get to feel success sooner and thus keep momentum up. If your smallest debt is not your highest interest debt, you may pay more in the long run than with the debt avalanche method, but with the debt snowball you can focus on a quick win to start your momentum.

Interest (Greatest to Least)

Ordering your debts by interest rate is sometimes called a debt avalanche. Really, it's just a variation of the traditional snowball method. In this case, you start with the loan of the highest interest rate, no matter the size of the loan. You still pay the minimum on all of your loans, but you put all of your extra toward the loan with the highest interest rate.

Ordering your debts by interest rate will save you more money in interest, especially if some of your loans have much higher interest rates than others. If you are not worried about having some early psychological wins, then this is the most logical mathematical option.

Choose the order that will work best for your personality and unique situation. Maybe you'll do a combination of the two. Depending on your individual situation, you might have additional factors that would lead you to choose to focus on a different debt first. Write down the order that you will pay off your debts.

Day 11 Challenge

Get all your debt recorded in one place and plan the order that you'll pay your debts. Be sure all of your minimum payments are covered in the budget you made on Day 7.

Day 12: Save Money on Gasoline

Since we don't pay separately for the fuel we use each time we drive the car, it's easy to keep ourselves blind to the actual cost of these trips. Since all our trips run together in our mind, when it's time to fill up we can't usually name any one trip as the culprit that drained the gas tank.

We may wish we didn't have to fill up, but what can be done? In most cases we can't just stop driving the car. If we go over our fuel budget but there's still a week left in the month, unless we suddenly decide to stay home from work, school, or church, we're pretty much forced to spend more than we planned. Gasoline seems like one of those expenses that we just have to suck up and pay, no matter the price.

While we don't have much control over the price of gasoline (besides choosing one station over another), there are lots of ways we can save money on gas by using less of it. Don't forget, every time you drive, you are also incurring real expenses in vehicle maintenance and time.

Here are a few great ways to save money on gasoline.

Combine Trips

We'll talk more about organizing time and trips on Day 13, but you may have already thought about how you can combine car trips to save time. A nice side effect is that it saves you a lot of money in gas!

Combining trips can mean two things. First, when you know you'll be going out, try to schedule other errands at the same time. Try to plan your trips to be geographically efficient. Hopefully you'll avoid driving back and forth across town. Second, combining trips means that instead of making three Target trips this week to pick up a few things each time, you'll keep a list of what you need so you can get it all in one trip!

Carpool

If you know someone else is headed the same direction, offer them a ride. Chances are you'll be on the receiving end the next time. Not only will you save gas, prevent wear and tear on your vehicle, be more environmentally friendly, and get to use the carpool lane, you'll also have good company!

A note of caution: For about a year, a friend's husband had been commuting 45 minutes with a female co-worker to save on gas. Sadly, that time together led to an affair and a divorce. No amount of money saved on fuel (or anything else) is worth jeopardizing your marriage! Be smart about who you ride with and don't put yourself in a compromising situation.

Take a Better Mileage Vehicle

If you have more than one car, be conscious of which car gets better gas mileage and use it whenever possible. We have a car and a van. The car gets 10 mpg more than the van, so when we just had three children we would take the car whenever we went out as a family. Just taking the car instead of the van to church on Sundays, I calculated our savings to be $145 per year.

Consider the Cost of Each Trip

Have you calculated how much a trip to the store costs you in gasoline? Consider that amount when you decide whether the trip is worth it or not. For example, if I know that a trip to Walgreens costs me $4 in gas, then it's easy to realize that making a trip there just so I can use my $2 off coupon to get a free item isn't worth it.

I don't like paying for shipping when I buy things online, but knowing that it costs me $9 for a round trip to Target (true story...we live in the boonies) makes shipping costs sound a lot more reasonable. Plus, with Amazon Prime, I don't even have to worry about shipping costs (not to mention standing in line, wrestling my kids, impulse buys, and being in the car for two hours).

If you're driving around town grabbing all sorts of free things people are giving away, you might want to rethink your strategy. It's easy to think, "Hey, it was free!" without taking into account that your old pickup gets terrible gas mileage. While the chase may be fun and sometimes yields great rewards, the prize often ends up just being more clutter at your house that will require a drive to the dump or the thrift store later down the road. Free stuff is great, but be selective. Don't start your engine at the first mention of a great deal.

Get Rid of Extra Weight

When you get back from your camping trip, take your Dutch ovens, tents, and coolers out of your trunk. Only keep what you absolutely need in your car. Remove extra racks and external storage when you're not using them.

Keep Tires Inflated

Keep your tires inflated to the recommended pressure. You can usually find the tire pressure recommendation on the inside of the door (near the hinge) or in the glove compartment. Check your tire pressure regularly, especially in cold weather. In addition to giving you better gas mileage, properly inflated tires will wear better, last longer, and be safer.

Drive Smarter

We all realize that idling, revving the engine, or peeling out when the light turns green uses more gas. A more subtle waste of gas is to keep the gas on when you could coast. Coast to slow yourself down instead of hurrying to a stoplight so you can slam on the brakes. Look down the road and time the stop lights so that you aren't always either on the gas or the brake.

Last Halloween we were at a party at a friend's house who lives 25 miles away. My husband met us there in his car after work. The van was completely out of gas (the "distance to empty" said 0 miles) and there wasn't anywhere open on our way home to get gas. Although there are some uphill spots on our drive, we live generally downhill from our friends (about 1,500 feet difference in elevation). Since my husband could drive behind us and we could all pile in his car if the van stopped, we decided to see how far we could make it.

I avoided using the gas or brake on our long downhills and would let the van coast uphill with its momentum. I wouldn't push on the gas until I absolutely had to. Since it was late at night in the boonies I didn't have to worry about anyone behind me when I was going slowly. Miraculously we made it all the way home! It made me realize that we can conserve a lot more gas by taking our time and "going with the flow." We are in a hilly area, so there are lots of opportunities to take advantage of this!

Walk or Ride Instead

For those of you who don't live in the boonies, some of the places you frequent are probably within walking or biking distance. When I was in college, I didn't have a car, but I didn't let that deter me from getting where I wanted to go. Walking or biking can also be a nice change of pace and a good excuse for some exercise!

Just Stay Home

As often as possible, try to stay home instead of driving around. This is a surefire way to save money on gas, but you might have to say no to some things or cut out some activities. The bright side is that you'll also find more time to cook from scratch, work from home, clean your house, play with your kids, and maybe even take a nap.

Taking Advantage of Low Gas Prices

When prices on food or other home goods hit rock bottom, it triggers our "stocking up" instincts. If you time things right and stock up on food when prices are low, you'll never have to pay full price. It's not so easy to stock up on low-price gas, but you can still cash in on the savings at the pump and have it make a big difference in your budget.

Just as important as saving money on gas is making sure that savings goes somewhere productive instead of getting lost in our checking account. If you don't budget, your gas savings will be lost in the shuffle. You probably won't notice the difference in your account balance because it's too easy to just spend the difference.

The way we have found to make sure our gas savings aren't lost is tied to how we budget down to zero each month, then use the excess in each category to go toward our financial goals (for now, finishing our student loans). The savings from cheaper gas prices don't just disappear into space, we notice them and we harness them because of the way we budget!

Day 12 Challenge

Resolve to reduce your gas usage in some way and aim the savings toward your financial goal!

Day 13: Get Organized to Save Money

There's no doubt that some people are just naturally more organized than others, but there's also no reason we can't each improve! Organizing both your space and your time will have an impact on how smoothly your life runs. When it comes down to it, being organized will save you money.

Let's look at some areas in our lives where improved organization will save us money. Be thinking about the changes that you can implement to become a little more organized.

Your Space

Have you ever sat down to work on a task, then kept having to get up to go find the things you need to complete it? Tackling a job without first organizing your space makes the job take longer and feel bigger, and is much less fulfilling than simply starting and finishing all in one sitting.

I will be the first to admit that I am not qualified to show you how to organize every inch of your house. I want to focus on one area of your house: where the finances happen. Maybe it's your office or computer desk. Maybe it's on your kitchen counter. Maybe you've got your financial stuff strewn throughout the house.

Here are some things to think about when organizing your financial space and stuff:

Designate a place for bills.

Keep all your current bills together. When bills come in the mail put them in their spot immediately. When you have your monthly budgeting meeting (we'll talk about that on another day), you will have them all together.

File old financial papers.

It's easy to let last month's statements and bills clutter the space for this month's papers. Create and use a filing system to take care of old statements, bills, and receipts. Maybe it's as simple as a single drawer you use. You may need to reference them later, but once they are paid, they should no longer be under your nose.

Your Time & Energy

Your time is precious. Your energy is limited. You will work faster and more efficiently if you are organized. With simple systems and organized habits you will save money and not waste valuable resources.

Here are a few ideas for being more organized with your time and energy:

Consolidate your activities.

Look at your calendar and plan your outings and flexible activities around activities that are already set. Think about your driving route to make your errands most efficient.

Plan a weekly (or monthly) menu.

Having an organized menu will save you money and sanity (which is priceless). We talked about planning a menu for cooking dinner at home, but you can do it for all your meals and snacks.

Make one trip to the grocery store.

When your menu is organized and you've planned a grocery list, you should be able to do all of your shopping at once for at least a week. If you've mastered that, try only going every two weeks. You'll save time, gas, and money.

Pay bills on time.

Set aside a day each month when you will pay all your bills. We do ours at our monthly budgeting meeting. I used to wait until the due date to pay credit card bills, thinking that by holding onto my money longer would earn me a little interest. Accidentally missing the due date and getting a late fee will more than negate any benefit for holding onto your money a little longer. Trust me!

Keep a shopping list.

In addition to a grocery list, keep a list of other household necessities. Keep your list on your phone or in a place where you have easy access. With an ongoing list, you'll be able to get what you need when you're at the store and won't have to make special trips for the things you forgot.

Day 13 Challenge

Like many of the challenges so far, you get to personalize this one to meet your specific needs. Choose an area where you are struggling to stay organized (maybe one of the bullet points listed above) and resolve to make the necessary changes to improve.

Day 14: Keep Budgeting Flexible

One reason budgeting gets a bad rap is that traditional budgeting often makes people feel like failures. When the month's spending doesn't match the amount you projected at the beginning of the month, it's easy to decide that budgeting just doesn't work.

Traditional budgets set spending levels in each category at the beginning of the month. This can be frustrating because those decisions feel rigid and unchangeable, at least for the month. It feels like cheating to increase a category limit midway through the month. When you set your grocery budget at $300 and end up spending $360, you feel like a budget failure. When in one month you go to both a wedding and a birthday party, and spend more than allocated on gifts, you wonder why you even try. Continually going over-budget causes discouragement, and discouragement makes people give up on budgeting altogether.

A flexible budget, on the other hand, allows for variations without ruining your bottom line or making you feel like a failure. When unexpected expenses come up or your priorities change, your budget should change accordingly. It's perfectly fine to change your category limits — it would be foolish not to.

With our flexible budget, we are confident that there will never be a single month that our expenses exactly match our beginning-of-the-month projections, and that's just fine. Flexible budgeting is not failed budgeting — it's realistic, guilt-free, liberating budgeting.

Keeping Your Budget Reliable

On Day 7 of *Frugal Fresh Start*, we covered the forward-looking budgeting method in which you allocate your actual, on-hand cash to your highest priority budget categories, consistently enter spending for those categories as you spend during the month, and check potential spending against the available category balance before making a purchase. (Remember, while we love YNAB, you could also use your own spreadsheet with YNAB rules and enjoy the benefits of the philosophy.)

Because you are budgeting with actual money rather than expected income, and recording expenses against the categories as you spend money during the month, you can implicitly trust your budget to show exactly how much is available in every category, every time you look at the budget. Your budget is a reliable indicator of your spending ability.

In YNAB, it's easy to ensure that your budget stays reliable. If you still have money to spend, the category balance shows green. If you have a red category balance, you have spent more than you had allocated to that category.

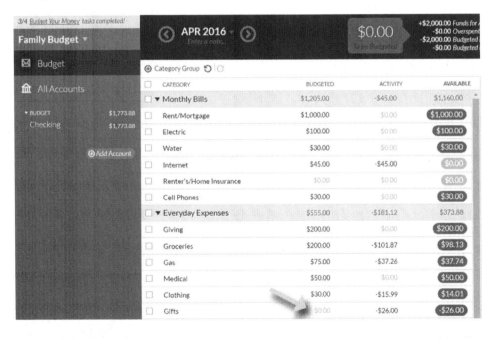

In the example above, you can see that no money was budgeted to the gifts category, so when $26 was spent on gifts, the category balance became red. The green category balances show categories with budgeted funds available.

When there is a red number in the third column, your budget is no longer reliable. You can't trust it to show how much you have to spend, because the over-spend in the red category has to come out of some other category. You need to change the budget to indicate which category needs to be decreased to account for the overspending. It's important to correct this as soon as possible by freeing-up money from other categories. Ideally you will look at your budget and make adjustments before overspending.

To resolve the overspending in the gifts category, $26 is taken from the budgeted amount in the medical category and budgeted to the gifts category instead.

Changing Category Allotments

Before spending money, we check our category balances (third column) to see if we have sufficient funds allocated for the proposed expense. If we do, we probably make the purchase. If we do not, we need to decide if this purchase is really a priority for us right now. If we decide that we need or want to over-spend in a category, we need to add other funds to that category before going through with the transaction. We can take unspent funds from another category and add it to the category where we need more funds.

Feeling Empowered

Remember that changing your category allotments and moving money around throughout the month is part of the plan. It's all about your priorities and being empowered to make decisions as they come up. Making changes multiple times every month is normal. It's not a big deal. There's no need to fret.

This is a healthy way to use your resources. An unhealthy way is to arbitrarily set a number at the beginning of the month, let those arbitrary number choices govern your priorities during the month, and feel like a failure when real life doesn't match your beginning-of-the-month guesses.

With flexible budgeting, you get all the benefits of living within your means (what budgeting is really about) and all the freedom to decide, guilt-free, what you want to do with those means as real life unfolds around you during the month. You get to make the choices, rather than being constrained by strict rules and untouchable category limits.

Reporting What Matters

When I first started "making personal finance public" by giving a monthly report of our actual earning, spending, and debt repayment at sixfiguresunder.com, I would share the amount that we had budgeted for each category as well as the actual spending. This is a normal approach for reporting a traditional budget. You can see how well your actual spending matches up with you projected spending.

Once we started using YNAB, I changed my reporting method. The amount we set on the first of the month isn't important. What is important is that as we make choices during the month, we keep our total spending lower than our total income, with as much allocated to debt repayment as our priorities allow.

Now I report how much we spend in each category, how we decided to make any unexpected spending changes, and how much we reduced our outstanding debt. Some months, as we roll with the punches, we end up spending more than we had projected in total, and end up with a lower debt repayment. Some months we spend less and pay off more debt. Every month, though, we set priorities, make initial projections, and then modify our budget to match our choices as real life meets our best guesses.

Just for the record, with categories like groceries, where our needs don't change much month-to-month (we still eat everyday), we do try to keep within our set $300 per month no matter what we might want to eat some days. It's kind of a fun challenge.

Day 14 Challenge

Look at your budget that you set up on Day 7. Are there any changes that you need to make? Don't hesitate to move money around if you need to. In the future, you can make changes (moving money from one category to another) as the need arises. Remember that your budget categories contain real money, so you should not spend more than is allocated to the category.

Day 15: Celebrate Your Progress!

Congratulations! You've passed the halfway point for the challenge!

Taking time to enjoy and celebrate your progress is an important part of staying motivated, especially for a goal that requires a change in habits and renewed self-control.

Most of your goals require you to give something up. That seems limiting and restrictive, maybe even punitive, until you remember that what you're really doing is buying back your freedom and peace of mind.

You're giving up what you want now for what you want most.

So let's celebrate how far you've come!

Look at What You've Done

Think through the past two weeks and the specific commitments and sacrifices you made to work toward your goal.

> 1. Set a Goal – You thoughtfully set an ambitious 6-month goal that will stretch you and make a meaningful difference in your financial health.
>
> 2. Cut Something Quick – You immediately began saving money by cutting one expense right out of your life.
>
> 3. Track Your Spending – You faithfully recorded every transaction for over a week now. As this practice becomes simple habit, you'll understand intuitively exactly what's happening with your money, and in understanding, you'll find your way to change.
>
> 4. Accountability – You found an accountability partner to share your goal with who can cheer you on and keep you from veering

off the path or backsliding. Hopefully, your partner knows of his new role.

5. Cook at Home – Despite your busy schedule and the fact that you're not a kitchen wizard, you have a workable plan to eat more meals at home, improving both your bottom and your bottom line.

6 & 7. Create a Budget – You've actually done it! You thoughtfully created categories, and then assigned your cash on hand to your highest priority expenses first, and then down the priorities as far as the cash reached. This is something you CAN live by.

8. Lower Your Bills – You ruthlessly examined your "fixed" expenses, and may have already made the calls that result in real savings, every single month.

9. Save Money on Utilities – You figured out ways that you can change your habits to reduce your utility usage.

10. Pack Your Lunch – You bucked the trend and brought your lunch from home. Secretly, all your friends and co-workers wish they could do the same.

11. Assess Your Debt – You took an honest look at your debts and made a plan of attack for eliminating them.

12. Save Money on Gas – You learned about and decided on ways that you can save money on transportation and put that money toward your goal.

13. Get Organized – You decided on some organizational improvements you can make to streamline your life and save you money.

14. Keep Budgeting Flexible – You know that a change in priorities doesn't have to wreck your budget. Now you can feel comfortable making changes to your budget throughout the month.

That's pretty impressive for a couple of weeks!

Celebrate Your Success!

It can be a little overwhelming sometimes, the idea of keeping all that up, and the thought of how much farther your still have to go. While you may feel like you have only inched toward your goal in the past two weeks, the reality is that you are creating great new habits that will pay off both in meeting this specific goal and in your long-term financial mastery.

How should you celebrate? That's completely up to you. It could be a simple splurge like going out for ice cream, or taking an evening off to do something enjoyable. Maybe you've been yearning for a little time to just read a good book by yourself. Maybe you've been intending to attend a child's basketball game. Maybe it's been years since you wandered through your favorite museum, or sat and sketched the view from your window. Maybe you just want to sit in front of a movie with your spouse instead of trying to think of ways to earn or save money. Whatever you choose, it should be a meaningful celebration for you. Let off some of the tension and do something that helps you enjoy the peace of mind you're earning with your hard work.

Don't forget to share with your accountability buddy so they can celebrate as well.

Day 15 Challenge

You have made awesome progress! Choose a favorite way to celebrate your success to date. Get together with your accountability buddy, your spouse or a friend, or treat yourself to an evening or afternoon alone doing something you love. After your celebration, decide what your next milestone will be, and how you will celebrate it. Now you have something else to look forward to!

Day 16: Frugalize Your Menu

First of all, pat yourself on the back for having a menu in the first place! If you're going strong on your challenge from Day 5 to cook at home, then you are off to a great start. That resolve alone will save you lots of money over eating out and getting premade food.

Today's challenge goes a step further into what to eat and what to avoid.

Now before I go any further, I should give the disclaimer that I'm not a dietician. I'm just a regular mom feeding a family of six on a budget. By all means, please adapt today's challenge to your family's dietary needs.

Eat meat sparingly

Depending on what you're used to, this can mean different things. For many people, having a "Meatless Monday" is a way to be more frugal. We go the opposite way. We will go meatless five or six days and have meat one or two days. Get protein from other sources like eggs, beans, nuts, yogurt, and cheese.

Eat fruits and vegetables in season

There's no reason why you can't buy fresh fruits and vegetables, even on a tight budget. They key is to buy what's in season. You can easily see what is in season by looking at the front page of the grocery store ad. The in-season produce will be what is lowest in price.

Pasta, potatoes and rice

Carbohydrates get a bad rap these days, but grains and starches are what have sustained generations of our forefathers for generations. They are filling and frugal. Instead of planning your meal around the meat, let your potatoes be the main dish, and use meat as the garnish or side. I try to alternate the base of my dinners between pasta, potatoes, and rice. That might sound boring, but with different seasoning, vegetables, and meat, you can make vastly different meals using the same base.

Soups and stews

Experiment with new recipes for soups and stews. Not only do they hit the spot on a cool fall evening, but they can be extremely frugal. Soups and stews are a great way to use leftover vegetables and smaller portions of meat. You can prevent a lot of waste in the kitchen by sticking any vegetables in the freezer before they go bad, then use them in your soups.

Hot cereal instead of cold

Cold cereal is expensive, it goes fast, and it's not very filling (though I must admit I love it, especially when I'm pregnant). Hot cereal, like oatmeal or cream of wheat, is much cheaper and it's more filling. To maximize your savings, avoid individual packets and buy in bulk instead.

Drink water

Not only is water essentially free, it's also much better for you than the alternatives. Serve water at meal times and throughout the day. If you want to feel fancy, add a slice of lemon!

Calculate the cost of your meals

You probably won't want to calculate the cost of all of your meals everyday, but having a basic grasp on how much a meal costs will help you to make your menu more frugal. It's also a good way to be aware of how much you're saving by eating at home. To calculate the cost of your home-cooked meal, simply add up the cost of the ingredients you use. Be sure to calculate the portion used for each ingredient. For example, if you use 1/3 of the block of cheese, use 1/3 of the price of the cheese. To compare meal costs by serving, divide the total cost of the meal by how many servings it makes for your family.

When you know the cost of a meal or the cost per serving, you can easily compare your family's favorite meals to see which are the most frugal. If you've never done this exercise before or thought about the cost of your meals, you might be surprised!

Day 16 Challenge

Look at your priorities when it comes to food and decide where you are willing to make changes. Maybe instead of having meat everyday, you can cut back to having meat only four days a week. Or, instead of making the meat itself the main dish, you can stretch your meat by incorporating it into a recipe like a stew, sauce or casserole. As in other challenges, you can tailor this one for your family.

Day 17: Make it Do

In the World War II era of victory gardens, saving kitchen grease, and donating scrap metal for munitions, the frugal slogan "Use it up, Wear it out, Make it do, or Do without!" became a nationwide mantra. Oh, how that has gone out the window today! Instead of using things up, we buy multiples in every color, style, model, and flavor. Instead of wearing things out, we throw them out (or they collect dust in our closets). Instead of making do, we make a fuss about how rough we have it. Instead of doing without, our credit cards are maxing out.

Our frugal forebearers would be appalled by our wastefulness.

Getting back to our roots by learning to "Use it up, Wear it out, Make it do, or Do without!" will challenge our current frugal (or not-so-frugal) habits. While we won't all go to the same extremes to save a buck, learning to work with what we have and not be wasteful can help us all to be more frugal.

Use It Up

My kids are always amazed at how I can always squeeze one more blob of toothpaste out of the tube. Leaving the near empty bottle of shampoo upside down always nets another day's hair-washing. With the help of a spatula (or "rubber scraper" as my husband calls it), you'll get another sandwich of peanut butter out of an empty jar. Does anyone else avoid the last two slices of bread in the loaf and let them go to waste?

Whether it's food, toiletries, or another limited resource, we probably all have room for improvement when it comes to "using it up." Maybe it means keeping the fridge more organized so produce and leftovers aren't wasted. Maybe it means making an extra effort to teach kids to not let their eyes get bigger than their bellies. Freezing leftover vegetable scraps is great for stew. Pressure cooking chicken or turkey bones makes great broth. Getting in a better habit of "using it up" will save us money and help us raise a less wasteful next generation.

My grandma is a frugal role model for me. Not only does she make use of everything as it was originally intended, she is a champion of reusing and repurposing things. While I spoil myself with nice food storage containers that I love, my grandma keeps reusing cool whip containers, pickle jars, and butter tubs. She saves the string, twist ties, and rubber bands from packages. If foil is still clean it can be used again.

Wear It Out

On their 50th wedding anniversary, my grandparents posed for a picture with the refrigerator (still working!) that they purchased when they got married. It's still going strong out in their garage (because my grandma is also the queen of stocking up). It's pretty safe to say that none of the fridges we are using today will be around in fifty years!

With most current appliances and electronics being built for a shorter expected life span, it shouldn't be too hard to "wear it out." On the one hand, many manufacturers "just don't make 'em like they used to." On the other hand, how often do we replace something because we lack the self-control to hold on to "just fine" when new models and updates keep rolling out?

When it comes to clothes, my in-laws are the epitome of "wear[ing] it out." They will wear clothes until they are absolutely threadbare. When the clothes start to show significant wear, they are designated as clothes for working in the garden or other dirty tasks until they are completely demolished.

It's understandable that not everyone (including me) wants to wear all of their clothes for decades until they are absolutely threadbare. There are lots of frugal alternatives for clothes, from passing them onto a friend or donating them to a thrift store, to selling them online or in a consignment shop.

Make It Do

"Need" is a very relative term. Almost every time that we (myself included) say that we "need" something, we would probably be fine without it. Sometimes we just might have to be a little more creative when it comes to a work-around. Not only does making it do build our character, we're also saving money and getting ourselves closer to our financial goal.

My grandma's antique fridge that's still keeping food cold after 50+ years, lost its handle a decade or two ago, but that wasn't a reason to get rid of a perfectly functional fridge. With a skilled hand and a screwdriver, the door pries open just fine.

Just to be clear, I'm not saying that you never buy anything new (or new-to-you). What I am saying is that too often we don't exercise any restraint or creativity when we "need" something. Next time you "need" something, try to think of how you can "make do" with what you already have!

Do Without

Even considering the things we all cut out in the beginning of the Frugal Fresh Start Challenge, we really don't "do without" the way our grandparents had to, or the way most of the world still does. We're pretty spoiled. Considering you're reading this on some electronic device, probably in your own home, vehicle, or workplace, I feel safe including you among the spoiled.

If we're worried about keeping up with the Joneses, going without will make us miserable. Focusing on our blessings and considering all we *do* have makes going without easier. Going without can be good for us and good for our kids. Are there some luxuries that you normally buy or were planning to buy that you could do without?

Day 17 Challenge

Give a second thought to upcoming purchases that are on your "to buy" list. Think about how you are managing without that item now. How can you "Use it up, Wear it out, Make it do, or Do without?" Could you make it do or do without until you reach the goal you set? Could you hold off and make that purchase part of your celebration for reaching a milestone?

Day 18: Involve the Kids in Finances

You are much more likely to be successful at reaching your goal when you're not doing it alone. That's why we've already talked about the importance of having a buddy or accountability partner.

Of course, getting your spouse on-board with the same financial goals is a huge win! Sometimes, however, we overlook the benefit of involving our kids in finances. In fact, in many cases we do our children a disservice by not involving them more in finances.

Sure, there are lots of arguments for not involving children in finances. We don't want to burden our children with adult problems like credit card debt or not enough income. We may think it's none of their business. We may be embarrassed to let them see our mistakes and shortcomings. We may just not have the patience to explain it all.

Bringing our kids into the process regarding finances has benefits, both long- and short-term. Kids learn through example– actions speak louder than words. If our kids follow our example (i.e. spending frivolously or living on loans) without knowing the big picture (i.e. drowning in debt), they're going to have to learn the hard way.

Being wise with money is a learned skill, which unfortunately isn't taught in schools. If they don't learn from their parents, children will have to rely on their own experience to teach them. Kids who learn to be smart about money from a young age will have a real advantage when it comes to the real world.

In my opinion, the benefits of involving kids in finances outweigh the drawbacks. Keep in mind, that what we share with our kids should be appropriate for their age. We don't need to reveal every last detail. We also don't need to be perfect in order to be effective teachers. It's okay for them to know that we make mistakes too.

Getting Kids Involved in the Family Goal

Whether your goal is to get out of debt, pay off your house, or save for a family vacation, your kids can be a part of it! Involving kids in your family's financial goals can help to unify your family. Talk to them about your goal and invite them to be on your team. Your excitement and enthusiasm (or negativity and pessimism) will be contagious! Tell them what changes you are making to reach the goal and let them know how they can contribute.

Here are a few do's and don'ts:

Do

- Let them know how they will benefit from the family goal.

- Tell them why you need their help.

- Explain specific ways that they can help.

- Notice and appreciate their efforts.

- Make it fun, like a game or a challenge!

- Involve them in celebrating milestones and other successes.

Don't

- Don't overwhelm them. Take their age and life experience into consideration.

- Don't give them more information than they need. Numbers and details can be burdensome for some kids.

- Don't make them feel guilty. Guilt is not a good or sustainable motivator.

Motivation to Make Sacrifices

Making changes to the way you spend money affects your kids. Maybe your kids are used to buying lunch at school and have to adjust to packing their own lunches. Maybe they are used to having fast food after soccer practice and will need to get used to waiting until they're home for dinner. If you cut cable to lower your bills, you can bet that your kids will notice! Any way you slice it, your kids are going to be affected by your choices to become more frugal.

Without knowing the reasons behind your frugal changes, kids are likely to become frustrated by the new habits you are trying to form. They may even be disgruntled enough to thwart your plan to change.

On the other hand, when your kids are involved in the family goal, they are motivated to make the necessary changes. They realize that you aren't just trying to make their lives hard; you're actually trying to improve their lives. Goals help to motivate all family members.

Keeping You Honest

Kids make great accountability partners—almost too good sometimes!

A few months ago we spent the entire day out and about. I had brought food with us for lunch, but I hadn't planned any food for dinner. We were an hour from home and I didn't have any plans at home either. I made the decisions to use the rest of the month's budgeted "fun money" to go through a drive-through for dinner.

Instead of being excited about this very rare occurrence, my kids were confused and disappointed. "Why are we buying food here? Don't we have food at home? I thought we were saving our money for Daddy's law school?" If I hadn't already ordered, I would have just gone home. The kids were trying to keep me on track!

Sharing in the Success

As part of the team, your kids will be able to share in the success of your goal, both in the end and along the way. They will feel that their sacrifices matter and are making a difference. Kids (and adults) are more likely to appreciate something that they worked hard to earn. By taking an active part in working toward the family goal, kids will learn the power and value of goal-setting. On top of that, they will be increasing their own financial skills and self-discipline, which will lead to future success on their own.

Day 18 Challenge

Think about how you can involve your children in your goal. What contributions can they make to be part of the team? How can you get them excited about your goal? Now go for it!

Day 19: Frugal Entertainment

Don't believe the myth that being frugal means you can't have any fun.

Whether you are looking for frugal entertainment temporarily while you work toward specific financial goals, or you want to change to a more frugal lifestyle, there are lots of great ways to have fun without spending a lot of money.

Community Events

Churches, community groups, schools, and college campuses are having events all the time and they are often free (and often include food). Look online for free local events and entertainment. You might be surprised at what's out there that you didn't know about.

If you plan ahead you can even get free or reduced admission to events that normally charge a fee. I learned that our county fair gives free admission to anyone who brings an entry for the daily food contest. My husband and I enter the daily food contest on the same day kids get in free and just like that we've got a free family activity!

Get Outside

One of our favorite forms of entertainment also happens to be absolutely free. We love hiking, camping, and exploring the outdoors. Most communities have well-maintained walking and biking trails that are free and very accessible. If you're like us and enjoy a more rustic experience, find a local or state park or forest near you. I even have an article on my blog that explains how you can camp for free, never paying for a camp site.

Bring Back the Potluck

What do we do when we get together with friends? We eat! Well instead of going to a restaurant and paying too much for food, have a potluck. Think beyond your church function or dinner at grandma's. Make potlucks fun by having a theme. You could have everyone bring their favorite Chinese dish and then produce chopsticks to eat with. You can make a potluck fun by having a contest. How about a chili cook-off!

Host an Event

Instead of going out, have others come to you! They'll probably appreciate the opportunity to save money on entertainment too. Don't feel like you have to provide all the food and entertainment either.

- If you have a barbecue, have everyone bring their own meat and a side dish to share.

- You could have a movie night where everyone brings a snack to share.

- If you have a projector (or know someone who does), head outside for a backyard movie on a summer night.

- Have a board game or video game competition along with a dessert bar.

Get a Deal on Your Entertainment

Group buy deal sites often have great dining and entertainment deals that are a fraction of the normal price. Plan your entertainment based on the deals you find. In addition to saving money, you'll also discover new places and events that you didn't know about. We've been able to add some new restaurants and events to our family favorites thanks to sites like Groupon and Living Social.

Be Sure to Plan Ahead

If you wait until Friday night to decide what you're going to do for the weekend, you're more likely to fall into old spending habits. Being frugal requires some planning, especially if frugality is a new habit for you. If you're hosting your own event, you'll need some time to prepare for it to be successful. You'll need to mark your calendar ahead of time so you don't miss out on the great free and cheap activities hosted in your community.

Day 19 Challenge

Write down a list of frugal entertainment options that you would enjoy. Look at your calendar and schedule one in. You might also consider making a list of non-frugal activities that you will avoid or limit.

Day 20: Save on Water

On Day 16, when I talked about frugalizing your menu, I suggested drinking water because it's "essentially free." I was careful not to say "free" because water isn't exactly free (though when we're talking about drinking water in a developed nation, the cost is pretty nominal).

Depending on the area where you live, water may be abundant and cheap, or limited and expensive. Changing the way you use water can make a difference in your budget. If you have a well, saving water also means saving electricity to run the well's pump.

There are many different ways to conserve water. Some actions take very little effort, while others are more challenging. Depending on your motivation, you can find at least a few changes that will work for you.

Simple Ways to Save Water

Turn off the water!

It sounds simple– and it is!– but many people don't do it. I've seen friends leave the kitchen water running down the drain while they rummage through the fridge or help a child with homework. The classic example of wasting water by not turning it off is when brushing your teeth. After you wet your toothbrush, turn the water off until you're finished brushing.

Get efficient!

A more efficient toilet can save 2 to 5+ gallons of water per flush. A low flow shower head can save up to 40% of the water an older model uses. Put a faucet aerator on all the faucets in your house. Shop for efficient water-using appliances like washing machines and dishwashers.

Use a dishwasher.

It doesn't take much to convince me to use a dishwasher instead of hand-washing dishes. Using an efficient dishwasher actually uses less water in most cases than a typical person hand-washing the dishes.

Run only full loads.

For both clothes and dishes, a full load is the most efficient way to go. Wait to run the dishwasher until it's full and make sure you have a full load of dirty clothes before you start the washing machine.

Don't wash clean clothes.

With a family of six, the laundry piles up in the blink of an eye. One of my pet peeves is finding clothes that I know were not even worn in the hamper. Sometimes they are even still folded. I've also been stressing to my kids that their pajamas are not dirty after being worn once and that their jeans can often be worn more than once too.

Hard Core Ways to Save Water

Take Shorter Showers.

Efficient shower heads still use two gallons of water every minute. That's a lot of water going down the drain. Try using a timer to help you cut down on the time you bask in the flowing warm water. You could even make short showers into a fun family shower challenge.

Shower Less Frequently.

Most people can still have good personal hygiene without a shower (or multiple showers) every day. In fact, in many cases, it's actually better for your skin to not shower daily. Personally I would rather take a longer shower less frequently than a short shower every day.

Recycle water.

Wash your produce over a bowl or bucket so you can use the water for your garden. Keep a bucket in the shower to collect the water as you're waiting for it to heat up. You can add the water to the washing machine or use it to water your plants or garden. The most hard core version of this would be to re-use all of the shower water by leaving the tub plugged during the shower and siphoning or pumping the full tub into a holding tank for later use. This water could be used to fill the toilet tank or water plants, depending on the soaps/shampoos you use.

Collect rainwater.

Rainwater can be collected and used to water your plants or garden. Your roof and gutter system concentrates all the water falling on the house into a few convenient downspouts. A barrel under the downspout is an easy way to save some of that runoff to use for outside watering. More complete catchment and filtration systems can be installed, but the cost starts mounting pretty quickly, so unless you're ready for a serious commitment, use buckets or barrels you already have or can find easily and inexpensively.

The good news is that no matter how terrible or terrific your current water usage habits are, there is always room for improvement. We've tried new ideas in recent years as we've been experiencing a years-long drought in our area.

Reducing the amount of water you use is frugal in more than just the money-saving sense. In addition to financial reasons for saving water, we want to conserve water for environmental reasons.

Day 20 Challenge

Decide what your family will do to save water. Your investment in today's challenge will vary depending on how much water affects your budget.

Even if you don't feel particularly compelled to conserve water, I encourage you to choose something you can do to save water. Even if it doesn't make a dent in your finances, it will increase your frugal mentality, which will extend to other areas in your life.

Day 21: Look Ahead in Your Budget

If your budget is tight and has always been that way, it might be hard to imagine thinking ahead about expenses before they arise. You're still drowning in what happened yesterday (or last month or last year). Having the foresight to plan for known upcoming expenses, or the possibility of unknown upcoming expenses, is one of the keys to getting out of the paycheck-to-paycheck cycle.

Hopefully, as you live within your budget by only spending money you actually have and lowering your bills and other expenses, you will begin to find more flexibility in your budget. As this happens, you will be able to plan ahead for future expenses so they don't set you back to square one (or worse).

Planning for Known Expenses

On Day 6, your assignment was to write down all of the budget categories you would need. We tried to brainstorm all the periodic expenses that we often forget until the bill arrives each year.

We want to think ahead about these expenses and start setting money aside for them so they don't catch us by surprise. The easiest way to do this is to divide the amount of what the total bill will be by the number of months you have to save for it. This is often referred to as a "sinking fund."

You don't need to move the money into a separate account (unless you really want to). It will be safe in your checking account as long as you're spending according to your categories and recording all of your spending.

Example: *Every September you pay $600 for your life insurance premiums. Assuming it's now January (but it's too late to squeeze it into the budget in January), you will have 8 months to save for this annual expense (Feb-Sept). Divide that $600 bill by 8 months,* *and you'll get $75. Each month budget $75 into the category for life insurance. The following year, you will have an entire 12 months to save up for your annual premiums, so you will only need to budget $50 each month toward life insurance.*

For some periodic expenses, you won't know exactly how much they will be. For example, property taxes might change from year to year. Looking at the previous year's expenses will usually give you a good idea of what to plan for. Since costs generally go up, it's a good idea to over-estimate what the expenses will be. Having money leftover will be nicer than not having saved enough.

Planning for Expected Expenses

In addition to annual and other periodic bills, we will probably have some expected expenses to save for even though we may not be sure when they will come or how much they will cost. Maybe you know that in the next few years your home will need a new roof. Perhaps your dentist has told you that your oldest daughter will need braces sometime soon.

If you drive an older car, you might want to start setting money aside for your next vehicle. Since you don't know when your car will die or will no longer be worth paying to fix, you don't know exactly how long you have to save. Choose an amount to set aside each month in your car fund. Even if you don't have quite enough set aside by the time you need it and you have to dip into your emergency fund, having some money saved can prevent financial hardship and borrowing.

Planning for Unexpected Expenses

Unexpected expenses can be an unprepared budget's worst nightmare. When a car suddenly needs expensive repairs or an illness requires costly medical procedures, we want our budget to be ready. I love having my budget prepared enough so we don't have to touch our emergency fund to cover the expense.

Preparing for unknown expenses requires some guesswork. You won't know how much future car repairs will cost or when they'll be needed. Looking at years past, you can estimate how much you generally spend on car repairs in a year, with the understanding that each year can vary greatly from the year before. Divide your average annual expense by twelve to get an idea of how much you should be setting aside each month for car repairs.

Just like expected expenses, having something to put toward these "emergency" expenses really will make a big difference, even if you don't have the full amount or still have to dip into your emergency fund. As the years go on, your experience will help you better estimate amounts to save for these sort of expenses.

Another Method

We followed the "sinking fund" method above for many years, long before we started our forward-thinking budget. We used to have many different savings accounts set up for each of our sinking funds categories. With our Capital One 360 online savings account, we could open as many separate savings accounts as we wanted. I thought having all the separate accounts was great until we changed budgeting methods.

Now, I love having the benefit of separate categories (instead of separate accounts) and not having to move money between accounts all the time. I can keep all of my money in the same account and not have to worry about it disappearing.

We actually do things a little differently since we are now in ultra-focused debt-payoff mode. Since we're generally putting over $2,000 toward student loans each month, even though our minimum payment is actually $0, we have some wiggle room. Instead of putting a chunk toward life insurance premiums each month, we put everything we haven't spent at the end of the month toward debt. On months where periodic or unexpected expenses come up, we just pay less toward debt.

I don't recommend this method for most people though. The reason this works for us is that we don't have a minimum payment and we are putting a big chunk of money toward debt each month. If we had minimum payments or were not on the fast track to pay off debt, we would definitely be back to using sinking funds.

Day 21 Challenge

Look ahead toward future expenses, known, expected, or unexpected and decide how much you will allocate to those budget categories. Refer back to the list of periodic expenses that you made on Day 6 to help you.

Day 22: Get it Used

A great way to become more frugal is to get things second-hand instead of buying them new. Anything you can buy new, you can also buy used. You just need to know where to look and how to look effectively.

Keep a List

The first key to effectively buying used is to keep a list. It may take longer to find exactly what you want when you're looking for it used. To combat this, I keep a running list of the things that I need and keep it with me. I try to think ahead about upcoming needs, so I'm not forced into a tight time frame. Then, whenever I'm at a thrift store or yard sale, I can focus on (and remember) my family's upcoming needs.

Even if I end up buying something new instead of used, putting the item on my list gives me time to think through the purchase and find the best deal instead of making an impulse purchase that I'll regret.

Here are some great places to shop for used things:

Yard Sales

Of all the options for buying used items, yard sales and garage sales are often the cheapest. People who regularly shop yard sales find amazing deals. The trouble with yard sales is that they really are hit and miss. Some days you'll find lots of treasures and other days you won't find a single thing. Depending on where you live, yard sales may be seasonal. They're also typically held on weekends, but don't have a set schedule.

Thrift Store

When you think of buying used items, the thrift store might be the first place that comes to mind. The great thing about thrift stores is they do have a set schedule, so you can shop them with more flexibility than yard sales. They have an ever-changing inventory, so you always have a chance of finding something great. Still, they are hit and miss.

Ebay

Ebay is the most well-known place to look online for second-hand treasures. Because you'll either have to pay for shipping or shipping costs will be figured into the price, you won't always get as low a price as you would at the yard sale or thrift store. The tradeoff is that you will easily be able to search from the comfort of your own home—no sifting through shelves and boxes, no driving from store to store.

Amazon

Some people don't realize that you can buy used items on Amazon too. When you search for books (and many other items) on Amazon, you have the option to see used items from other sellers. Amazon will show the available items listed in order of total price (price plus shipping) so it's easy to compare prices.

Online Consignment Shops

When it comes to clothing and accessories, there are many online consignment and boutique options. If you're looking for a specific item, it's really nice to use their search features to find what you're looking for rather than sift through racks at a thrift store. My favorite place to buy clothing online is ThredUp. While the prices are cheaper than the same items new, you'll only find high quality top brands, so the cost is more than what you'd find at a thrift store.

Craigslist

Craigslist.org is a great place to find used items locally. It's been around for a long time and is used by a wide variety of people. You can find everything from cars to furniture to baby clothes. It's convenient to be able to search for and browse items you're looking for without leaving home. You can email or call sellers to ask questions, negotiate prices, and plan a time and place to meet up. Use caution when meeting to look at or buy an item from someone you don't know. Meet in a public place and don't give out personal information.

Local Facebook Groups and Varage Sale

Facebook has local buy/sell/trade or virtual yard sale groups where you can search for used items. Like Craigslist, you have the benefit of searching from the comfort of home without having to factor in the price of shipping. Facebook has the added perk of having a name and face to go with the person you're going to be meeting up with, so there is a little more social pressure than on Craigslist.

Many local Facebook groups have switched to using VarageSale. You login to VarageSale using your Facebook credentials, but the website is designed to be more convenient to search, buy, and sell than a Facebook group. The buyer and seller leave ratings for each other, so there is more incentive to be honest and not flake out.

Things I Wouldn't (Usually) Buy Used

Although most things can be purchased second-hand without a problem, there are some things you'll want to avoid buying used or at least be extra cautious about. A lot of this is my personal preference. What you do and don't mind buying used may vary, but maybe this will give you some ideas of usable used items you hadn't thought of.

Mattresses

I'm squeamish when it comes to used mattresses. Between the normal sweat, skin cells, and dust mites, the mattress has collected bodily fluids (from people and pets) and maybe even bed bugs. Ewww.

When we got married, we bought a new queen mattress and box spring from a college student who had a business selling them wholesale from a storage unit. It cost us $300 and ten years later we are still sleeping on it.

When we needed three twin mattresses for the triple bunk beds that my husband built for Christmas, we were thrilled to find very affordable new ones on Amazon that work perfectly for the kids.

Underwear

I'm actually fine buying kids underwear used and cloth diapers used, but I draw the line at adult underwear. Thrift stores sell them, so I know some people buy them; I just don't.

Pillows

While some pillows can go in the washing machine, I generally have the same concerns with pillows that I have with mattresses.

Car Seat

A car seat is probably the number one baby item that people will insist you should buy new so that you know it isn't expired and has never been in a collision. If you get a car seat from someone you know and trust, then I wouldn't hesitate to get a used one.

Things from a Smoker's Home

It's not just clothing and upholstery that absorb the tobacco smell. Wood, plastic, and other materials also soak up the smoke smell and are nearly impossible to freshen up.

I bought a beautiful kitchen island from a yard sale during our law school years. Since the sale was outside, I didn't notice that it came from a smoker's home. As soon as I got it in my home, the smell was very apparent. I tried everything to get rid of the smoke smell–leaving it for days in the sun, scrubbing with vinegar, scrubbing with bleach, even repainting. I learned to give everything I buy the sniff test before making a purchase. If I'm buying online, I always ask the seller ahead of time.

Day 22 Challenge

Think of some items that you'll be buying in the near future. Make a plan for how you will shop used items first.

Day 23: Do It Yourself (or Don't)

The phrase "do it yourself," or DIY for short, means taking back the responsibility for something that you would otherwise buy or hire out.

DIY projects are all the rage these days. With a desire to be more natural and get back to basics, many people are interested in discovering ways to be more self-reliant.

The internet is loaded with tutorials for doing things yourself. Pinterest is filled with all of the homemade cleaning and personal care products you can imagine. Images of home décor and home improvement projects abound.

In addition to the projects you can do and products you can make yourself, there are also chores or services – like getting a haircut or changing the oil in your car – that you can choose to hire out or do yourself to save money.

There is a notion that frugal people do things themselves rather than buying or hiring out. Doing things yourself has the potential to save you lots of money, but that's not necessarily the case.

Is it Worth it?

I love DIY projects, but even when I'm being careful, they sometimes don't always turn out as frugal as I had hoped. While frugal and DIY can sometimes be synonymous, they aren't always. Be careful of the DIY projects you undertake. Here are some factors to think about:

Time

Time is usually the biggest trade-off when you choose to do something yourself instead of buying or hiring out. How long will the project take? Do you have time to do it yourself? What is the opportunity cost? If you have options to do work that pays more than the DIY project would save you, then working might be a better use of your time.

Costs

Time is not the only factor that goes into figuring out if something is cost effective. You also need to consider the supplies or ingredients necessary for the undertaking.

Desire

DIY projects take work, plain and simple. If it's not something that you want to do, you may burn out before you get to reap any of the benefits from your efforts. At the same time, it's okay to do hard things that aren't necessarily enjoyable in order to save money, learn skills, or build character.

Skills

Is this DIY endeavor something you know how to do already or do you need to learn and practice before you can really do it yourself? Thanks to the internet, you can find videos and tutorials to teach you how to do just about anything. Still, learning a new skill takes time and practice.

Other Reasons to DIY

Of course not all DIY projects are done in order to save money. There may be some DIY projects that don't save you money, but you do for reasons of expressing your creativity, customizing something, or being more natural. For example, maybe it's not necessarily cheaper to make your own shampoo but you do it anyway to avoid chemicals.

At sixfiguresunder.com I give a cost breakdown for some of the DIY projects I choose to take on, like haircuts or making my own yogurt or laundry detergent, but you have to decide if it's worth it for you. Our choices in what we do ourselves and what we buy or hire out take so many factors into consideration. The decision is a completely personal one that often goes beyond cost.

Day 23 Challenge

Today's challenge is two-fold. First, look at the services that you currently hire out (oil changes, haircuts, lawn care, etc). Are there any of those that you could do yourself to save money?

Next, are there any products (i.e. laundry detergent) or projects (i.e. home improvements or auto repairs) that you would be interested in doing yourself? Do research on their cost-effectiveness and make plans to give one of them a try.

Day 24: Own Your Frugal Fresh Start

As you change your habits, those around you will start to notice. When you suddenly turn down your co-workers' daily invitations to lunch or sell your latest iPhone and its expensive plan to get on a more economical one, people will notice.

Depending on what your pre-frugal life was like, there is a good chance you will be challenged, or even teased, for your newfound frugality. Don't take it personally! Be proud that your change was big enough to be noticed. Secretly they are probably wishing they had the guts and determination to make the financial strides you're making.

Stop Playing the Victim

When approached about the frugal changes you've made, you might be tempted to say, "I just can't afford to eat out anymore" or "I can't go out to lunch anymore." Words like that make you the victim. They make you powerless and pitiable.

One way to own your frugal fresh start is to avoid talking like a victim. You have to be the one calling the shots and making the choices. Your words need to reflect that. When you say, "I can't afford that" you are not acknowledging that you have a choice in the matter. Instead you blame your circumstances.

When you're invited to go out, but you'd rather stay home and save your money for something else (i.e. your goal), don't use the "I can't afford that" cop out. Instead say, "I'm working toward a huge financial goal right now, so I've decided not to spend money on anything extra." Whatever you say, make sure you acknowledge that you are making a choice not to spend money.

Don't be a slave to your budget. You are the master. You are the one who is making the choice of where to put your money. Don't blame the budget.

Own It

When you own your frugal fresh start, you acknowledge that you have a choice in the financial decisions you make! You could go out to eat, but you choose not to. You could buy new furniture, but you choose to use that money for something else.

Giving up what you want now for what you want more is hard, but learning to make sacrifices is key to your financial success. In a world of indulgence, self-control is a characteristic that must really be learned and practiced.

While initially you might feel embarrassed or resentful of your new frugal ways, once the moment passes, you will be happy that you didn't give in. The more you stand up for yourself and your financial choices, the easier it will be.

At the end of the day, you will be respected, by yourself and others, for taking responsibility for your choices

Day 24 Challenge

Think about the situations that have come up (or will potentially come up) that will require you to own your frugal fresh start. It might be facing a co-worker or a family member who is always inviting (or tempting) you to spend money. Maybe there is someone who gives you a hard time about the little things that make up a big part of getting your finances in order. Perhaps you are your own worst enemy and the arguments happen inside your head.

Have some mental role plays where you take ownership of your newly-found frugality. What can you say that shows you are taking responsibility for your financial choices rather than playing the victim? Think of how you will respond when challenged or tempted. Write down a few responses that include words like "I'm choosing…" or "My priority right now is…." Try them out aloud a few times and look for the first time you can use them in real life.

Day 25: Frugal Gifting

It's the thought that counts.

We've all heard that before, but how many of us believe it? Do our gift-giving practices reflect what really matters or are we caught up in the price (or perceived price) of our gift? If we get caught up in the cost of our gifts, are we really paying attention to the meaning?

You might wonder what this has to do with frugality. You might just think I'm advocating skimping on your gifting budget. Before we go any further, let me clarify what I mean by "frugal gifting."

What is Frugal Gifting?

Being frugal in gift-giving is not synonymous with giving cheap gifts. A frugal gift is a gift that is a practical, thoughtful gift that is given from the heart, but within your means.

The problem most people have is the last phrase: "within your means." When we perpetuate rules on the monetary value that a gift for a certain occasion should have, then we aren't necessarily giving a gift within our means.

For some people a $75 wedding gift easily fits into their budget, but for our family on a tight budget, that sum represents more than a week's worth of groceries. My point is that you need to decide your own gift-giving budget standard rather than adopt what "everyone else" says is acceptable.

Instead of spending a lot of money, we aim for gifts that are thoughtful and useful. Here are some tips for giving great gifts:

Ideas for Giving Great Gifts

Something Useful

I think it's safe to say that most people have more dust collectors, trinkets, and decor items than they know what to do with. In a society that is accumulating stuff at a tremendous rate, we should focus on giving gifts that are useful.

Something You Love

When you have a product or service that you love, it's natural to want to spread the word and share it with others. Being able to stand behind a gift with a personal conviction that it's wonderful means so much to the recipient.

Something Personal

Giving something personal takes more time and thought than just buying something. Whether it's putting together a photo book full of memories, writing a love letter to your spouse or parent, or assembling a cookbook of favorite family recipes, your personal and thoughtful gift can't be matched by something store bought.

Something Handmade

While not everyone is a talented artisan, experienced seamstress or creative cook, if you do have special skills, handmade items make wonderful, thoughtful gifts. Handmade gifts aren't necessarily less expensive than store-bought gifts, especially when time is considered, but they allow you to give a piece of yourself in a way that store-bought gifts don't.

Something Consumable

With as many gift-giving occasions as there are, it can be nice to receive gifts that can be used up or consumed, rather than add to a mountain of stuff and create clutter. Consumable gifts are great for neighbors, teachers, or the person who already has everything.

Give Within Your Means and Don't Be Ashamed

Giving gifts that your finances don't allow won't bring happiness. While it may feel exciting in the moment of purchasing or giving an extravagant gift, eventually the credit card bill will roll around or other financial obligations will go unmet. It is not worth getting those fleeting moments of gift-giving pride when you're left with regret for overspending.

Staying within your budget will make the recipient more comfortable too. Receiving a gift that was clearly out of the giver's budget can be awkward for the recipient.

Never be ashamed of a thoughtful gift that you have given with love. Don't be embarrassed if it doesn't measure up to society's monetary standard.

Day 25 Challenge

Look ahead on your calendar for upcoming gift-giving occasions. Decide what you will budget for gifts. What can you do to keep your gifts within your means, but still be sure they are thoughtful and sincere?

Day 26: Hold Monthly Budget Planning Meetings

It may not sound fun, romantic, or exciting, but I have to admit that I really look forward to our monthly budget planning meeting. We treat it like a date! The kids are in bed and we're together focused on the same thing. We're on the same team working to achieve goals. Seeing our progress, reaffirming our goals, and making sure we're on the same page is motivating and fun!

Before I lay out the way we do our monthly budgeting meetings, I want to be clear **that there is no one right way to do your budget planning meetings**. The important part is that you are doing it! We have ours monthly, but you might want to do them more often (I think they should be at least monthly). You are checking in and holding yourself accountable. You're tweaking, making improvements, and celebrating progress. The details and agenda will vary according to your personal situation and goals.

Here's a peek inside our budget planning meeting. You'll notice that it is focused around our goals, which are currently heavily weighted towards debt-payoff.

Reconcile

Before we assess our progress on our goals, we have to make sure all of our numbers are right. We want to make sure that our accounts (transactions and totals) match what we have in our budget in YNAB.

Reconciling with two people is pretty convenient (though it's totally doable on your own too). I'm usually at the desktop computer with our budget open and my husband is on his laptop with each of our accounts open. We go through our checking account, and each of our credit cards with my husband reading off all the transactions and me marking them as cleared in YNAB. Then we compare our totals.

It's really fun when the numbers match up just right and we can reconcile immediately. Sometimes we'll find that we forgot to enter a transaction or there's one that's entered twice, or we transposed some numbers or something else that requires a little detective work before the account reconciles. It's probably nerdy to admit that it's fun either way, so I won't.

Pay Bills

While my husband is in each of our credit card accounts, he pays the bill. One of my favorite parts of using YNAB is that we don't have to worry if there is enough money in the checking account to cover the bills because when we "spend" the money from our categories it stays in the bank just waiting for the bill to come.

Two of our credit cards earn points that we redeem for "cash" or statement credits. They don't have a certain threshold that has to be reached in order to use them, so we apply the cash back each month before paying the card. Since we have all the money on hand to pay our credit cards each month, the cash back essentially goes straight to our debt repayment! For those curious about how we work that in YNAB, we enter the cash back as income for that month (instead of the next month, like we do for all of our other income), then it's funneled into our "end of the month payment" category.

For those who are new to YNAB, remember to record your money transfers (i.e. paying your credit card bills) so that YNAB shows that the money goes out of your checking account (outflow) and goes in to your credit card account (inflow). When you make that single transfer it will show up both under your checking account and your credit card when you look at them individually.

Re-Distribute

After we make sure our accounts match YNAB and pay our bills, we go through and add any extra money left in our categories to our end of the month debt payment category. You can read in detail about our personal approach to maximize our end-of-the-month payment if you want to see the explanation with screenshots. You could leave the money in those categories and roll them over into next month (like we talked about on Day 14), but our primary focus right now is paying off debt, so we empty our categories each month.

Make Our End-of-Month Debt Payment

When everything is re-distributed and the category balances (third column) are at zero, we pay the remaining lump toward our debt (our end-of-the-month debt payment)! Depending on how the month went, sometimes it's small, but it's always worth celebrating! Before we used YNAB, we didn't have an end-of-the-month debt payment at all because we had no idea how much we could spare.

Update our Debt Spreadsheet

While my husband is signed into the student loan servicing site to make the end-of-the-month payment, we record the payoff amount of each of our loans. You would think there would be some place where you could get a total like that (how much you owe total, plus interest), but there isn't. Since they make it inordinately difficult to know how much you really owe, we keep track on our own spreadsheet and update it each month. We have caught mistakes and inconsistencies in their records, so it is worth tracking. I make note of our "total paid in debt" and "total debt remaining" to post in our monthly reports on the blog.

Budget and Goals for Next Month

Since we are living on last month's income, we can budget (allocate money to our categories) for the entire next month. If you aren't to that point yet, you'll just fund your categories each time you get paid.

After we fund our categories, we decide what our beginning-of-the-month debt payment will be. We usually make it a pretty good chunk of what we have remaining unbudgeted. We tentatively leave the rest in our end-of-the-month debt payment category, which gives us some flexibility for unexpected expenses.

We pay the beginning-of-the-month chunk toward debt and start getting excited about the month. We review our goals and get pumped to spend as little as possible so that we can put more toward our debt at the end of the month!

A Few Key Points to Remember

• Couples, remember that you're on the same team! Work together. Build each other up. Don't point fingers of blame.

• Make it fun! Seeing your progress and working to stay on track is a positive thing. And if just having your budgeting meeting isn't exciting enough, pull out a carton of ice cream and two spoons (that always works for at least one of us)!

• Focus on your progress! In order for budgeting meetings to be sustainable, they need to be positive. Of course you will see areas that need improvement, but don't dwell on your shortcomings.

• Get excited about your goals! I always come away from our monthly meetings with renewed hope and motivation.

Day 26 Challenge

Set a date, time, place, and agenda for your next budget meeting. Let your spouse know that there will be refreshments served, so it's an event he or she won't want to miss! If you're spouse- and partner-free, invite your accountability buddy and celebrate together.

Day 27: Don't Give Up Giving

We've talked about lots of ways to be frugal and save money. We've also talked about meticulously managing our money so it doesn't disappear (funny how that happens). Before we're through, I wanted to touch on giving.

Don't *not* give in the name of frugality. Being frugal isn't just about spending less money. Frugality is about being intentional with your money. Choosing to give is definitely an intentional use of money, one that I don't want to overlook, so today we'll talk about how you can (and why you should) give generously even when finances are tight.

Why should I give when finances are tight?

Let's start with the "why" since the "how" is only important once you have a "why."

Why should you give when you're on a tight budget? Why should you give at all? That may have an intuitive answer for some people and might be a soul-searching question for others. I'm not here to judge your conclusions, just to encourage you to ponder and discover your own answers. Here are some common reasons people give, both of their resources and time.

To support causes that matter to us

You've probably heard the saying, "put your money where your mouth is." We can talk all day about things that matter to us, but it's when we start doing something about it (i.e. giving of our money, time, and resources) that we show our true devotion.

We feel that we should

Because of religious beliefs, many feel compelled or commanded to give. While it may be difficult to explain this to non-believers, those who give for spiritual reasons are content doing so because it is "right" and because they feel blessed for giving.

It feels good

If you are feeling down and out, one of the best ways to snap out of it is to go serve someone else. You'll look at your own problems in a new light. You might even be glad that you have your problems and not someone else's. It's kind of magical—doing good feels good.

Generosity is a habit

We are creating habits every day. If you're not giving, you are strengthening the habit of not giving. It's easy to say, "When I make more (or when my debt is paid, or when our house is remodeled), I will be generous." Having more money (or less debt) is not going to make us suddenly generous. We need to cultivate the habit of giving now.

How can I give when finances are tight?

Make giving a priority

If you've decided that giving is important to you, then make it a priority. Budget money for giving just like you would budget money to another priority. As you do it, it will become easier.

Give of your time and talents

Money isn't the only thing you have to give. In many cases, time is even more precious than money. If money is tight (and even if it isn't), volunteering is great way to give. Whether you're giving your time to serve in an organized community project, or you're taking time to help an elderly neighbor repair his home, giving of yourself is a great way to give.

Give of your stuff

Donating things (not junk), is another way to be generous when your monetary resources are limited. You can donate to a non-profit thrift store or offer what you have to give on Freecycle.org or Craigslist.org. You aren't limited to second-hand goods. You can use your time, talents, and stuff to make dinner for a neighbor or sew clothes for premature babies.

Making room in your budget for giving is not a new financial principle. If you have read any books on personal finance, chances are good that you have heard the case for not giving up giving. While the information and ideas may not be new, you can look with new eyes this time around on your Frugal Fresh Start journey!

Day 27 Challenge

Decide how you can work giving into your budget or schedule.

Day 28: Create Frugal Habits

You made it! You stuck with me for the whole Frugal Fresh Start Challenge! Pat yourself on the back! I hope you feel energized with ideas and motivation to pull you through reaching the goal you set back on Day 1 of the challenge. You can do this!!

Now What?

If you haven't taken the time to implement all of the money-saving strategies we've talked about, take some time and go back through the days and complete the challenges you missed. For example, lowering your bills (Day 8) might take more than a day to thoroughly complete if you give each one an honest-to-goodness try.

I tried to stick with basic, fundamental areas where most everyone can save money, but surely there are many more that would apply specifically to your situation. I am continually sharing ideas on my blog, SixFiguresUnder.com, to help you be even more frugal.

For example:

• If you're a household of one or two, you might look into tips for cooking for one or two.

• If you're expecting, you'll be interested in ways to save money on pregnancy.

• If you have kids, you can see how to get kids clothes free or cheap.

• If you are a college student (or have kids who will be heading off to school soon), you'll want learn frugal tips for college students.

Create Frugal Habits

The key to continued success is creating frugal habits. Some of the challenges this month were probably new to you. Maybe you had never tracked your spending or made a budget before. Maybe you never considered the impact of eating at home or the ways you could save money on gas. I'm sure we all have many areas where we can be more frugal and put more money toward our goals.

Don't let that overwhelm you.

Decide on a couple of areas (or just one, if you're feeling overwhelmed) where you can really improve. Focus daily on making this into a habit. Enlist your accountability buddy to help keep you on track. Don't give up! You can do this!

You still have five months left to work toward your six-month goal. You can do this!!

Staying Accountable Together!

I wanted a place where readers can share goals, struggles, and progress regarding frugality and finance, so I started a private Facebook group for readers. We've already had some great discussion over there!

If you're interested in a being a part of a supportive community that is encouraging and full of great ideas, you can sign up to get the details here: **sixfiguresunder.com/ffs-list** . It's a great way to stay accountable and cheer each other on!

You can also get my email newsletter to get a weekly dose of real-life encouragement for your Frugal Fresh Start journey. To sign up, go here: **sixfiguresunder.com/newsletter** .

Day 28 Challenge

Think back through your Frugal Fresh Start and go back to any topics that you didn't complete. Also, thinking about your six month goal that you set on Day 1, what habits do you need to change or keep up in order to reach your goal? Determine to form these habits!

Resources and Recommendations

A complete list of the blog posts referenced in this book, as well as the recommended products and services, can be found here:

http://www.sixfiguresunder.com/ffs

Additionally, you can request an invitation to join the private Facebook group where readers discuss and encourage one another on topics of finance and frugality by signing up here:

http://www.sixfiguresunder.com/ffs-list

That's also the place to sign up to receive updates on the information in this book.

About the Author

Stephanie Jones and her husband live in the boonies of northern California with their four kids ages one to eight. When she's not crunching numbers for the family's finances, you can find her adventuring outdoors with the family, sewing something fabulous for the kids, or baking something delicious.

At SixFiguresUnder.com, Stephanie shares her family's journey to pay off over $130,000 of law school student loans. Each month she openly shares what her family earns, spends, and pays toward debt.

You can find her on social media here:

- ➢ Pinterest.com/SixFiguresUnder

- ➢ Facebook.com/SixFiguresUnder

- ➢ Twitter.com/SixFiguresUnder

Made in the USA
Lexington, KY
09 March 2018